CW00525456

THE SIEGE OF COLCHESTER.

ESCAPE OF LORD CAPEL.

THE
SIEGE OF COLCHESTER;

OR,

AN EVENT OF THE CIVIL WAR, A.D. 1648.

BY THE

REV. GEO. FYLER TOWNSEND, M.A.,

Author of " The Sea Kings of the Mediterranean."

· · ◄━━ · ·

PUBLISHED UNDER THE DIRECTION OF
THE COMMITTEE OF GENERAL LITERATURE AND EDUCATION,
APPOINTED BY THE SOCIETY FOR PROMOTING
CHRISTIAN KNOWLEDGE.

━━◆━━

The Naval & Military Press Ltd

Published by

The Naval & Military Press Ltd
Unit 5 Riverside, Brambleside
Bellbrook Industrial Estate
Uckfield, East Sussex
TN22 1QQ England

Tel: +44 (0)1825 749494

www.naval-military-press.com
www.nmarchive.com

PREFACE.

THE annals of history record many sieges of pre-
eminent renown, as the sieges of Syracuse, Saguntum,*
and Jerusalem. The Great Civil War in England
was memorable for its sieges of Gloucester, Hereford,
and Pontefract, which have received ample notice
from historians. The famous siege of the city of
Londonderry has been immortalised by the narrative
of its chief hero, the Rev. George Walker. Many
persons in our own days have witnessed the brilliant
efforts of Sir William Fenwick Williams at Kars, or
have wept over the excruciating tribulation of our
countrymen and countrywomen at Lucknow. The
scenes related in this book may claim a comparison
with any of the preceding, in the chivalry of the
courage, the splendour of the achievements, the patience of the endurance, and the bitterness of the
privations of those engaged in them.

The siege of Colchester, the chief event in the

* This siege gave rise to a proverb commemorative of the severity of
its famine—Saguntina fames.

A

second civil war, A.D. 1648, is remarkable for a variety
of circumstances: for its long continuance; for the
extent of its entrenchments, redoubts, and fortifications; for the inequality of the combatants; for
the unflinching and determined courage of both
parties in the fight; for an almost superhuman endurance of privations; and for the final summary
vengeance, and severe retribution inflicted by the
conquerors on the conquered. With sympathies and
prepossessions strongly enlisted on the side of the
Royalist defenders of Colchester, the author has done
full justice to the courageous and valiant acts of their
opponents. He has neither diminished the lustre of
their success, nor discoloured any statement by
malice, partiality, or exaggeration. He now pub-
lishes this narrative in the double hope, that he may
contribute to a better understanding of an important
and most interesting crisis in English history; and
that he may promote a wider knowledge of daring
deeds, of personal sacrifices, of noble resolutions, of
high-souled principles, of honourable actions performed
by English gentlemen in days gone by in behalf of
their country and their king, and which are yet
worthy of perpetual commemoration and imitation in
all succeeding generations.

CONTENTS.

CHAPTER I.

HOW IT CAME TO PASS THAT COLCHESTER WAS BESIEGED.

CHAPTER II.

FROM THE COMMENCEMENT OF THE SIEGE TO THE FIRST INVESTMENT OF THE TOWN.

A 2

CHAPTER III.

THE IMPRISONMENT AND RELEASE OF SIR WILLIAM MASHAM.

CHAPTER IV.

A WORD ABOUT THE "BAYS" AND "SAYS" MAKERS.

CHAPTER V.

FROM THE FIRST INVESTMENT OF THE TOWN TO THE
CAPTURE OF ST. JOHN'S GATEWAY, AND THE
BURNING OF THE SUBURBS. FROM JUNE 30TH
TO JULY 16TH.

PAGE

CHAPTER VI.

A CHAPTER ON MILITARY AFFAIRS.

CHAPTER VII.

DIURNAL OF SIEGE—FROM THE CAPTURE OF ST. JOHN'S
GATEWAY AND THE BURNING OF THE SUBURBS, TO
THE TERMINATION OF THE SIEGE—FROM JULY 16TH
TO AUGUST 27TH.

CHAPTER VIII.

THE MORROW OF THE SURRENDER.

Arrangements for the cession of the town—Places assigned for the
    surrender of horses, arms, officers, and lords—Escape of Colonel
    Farre—Triumphal entry of Sir Thomas Fairfax—His success
    not an unalloyed satisfaction—Council and discussion at the
    Moot Hall—The condemnation of three knights—A solemn

CHAPTER IX.

THE PASQUINADES OF THE SIEGE.

CHAPTER X.

THE FURTHER PROCEEDINGS OF FAIRFAX.

CHAPTER XI.

THE FINAL RETRIBUTION.

CHAPTER XII.

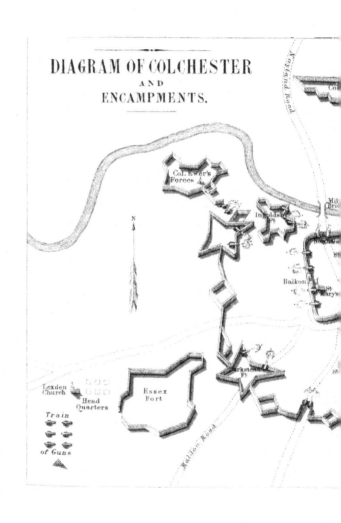

DIAGRAM OF COLCHESTER
AND
ENCAMPMENTS.

Col. Ewer's Forces

Ingoldsl...

Balkon...

Lexden Church

Head Quarters

Train

of Guns

Essex Fort

...rkst...

Malton Road

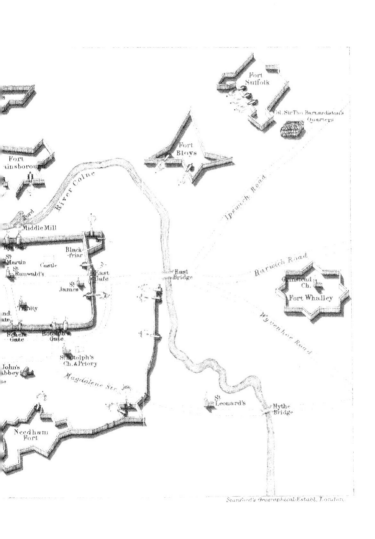

Fort Suffolk

Col. Sir Tho. Barnardiston's Quarters

Fort Bloys

River Colne

Fort Rainsborough

Ford

Middle Mill

St Martin

St Runwald's

Black-friar

Castle

East Gate

St James

Ipswich Road

East Bridge

Harwich Road

Grimstead Ch.

Fort Whalley

Trinity

...d.
...ate

Scotch Gate

Botolph Gate

St Botolph's Ch. & Priory

John's Abbey

Magdalene Str.

Wyvenhoe Road

St Leonard's

Hythe Bridge

Needham Fort

Stanford's Geographical Establ. London

THE SIEGE OF COLCHESTER.

CHAPTER I.

HOW IT CAME TO PASS THAT COLCHESTER WAS BESIEGED.

" The arms are fair,
When the intent of bearing them is just."
SHAKESPEARE.

The year 1648 a memorable year—Prodigies seen at its commencement
—Aspect of political affairs—Circumstances which led to the siege
of Colchester—Its sudden occupation by the Royalists—Defeat of
Fairfax before its walls—Comparison of the two contending armies
—The number of the forces of Fairfax.

THE year of grace 1648 was a very memorable era in
English history. Its commencement was ushered in
with reports of unusually strange sounds* in the air,

* On the 28th day of February, "several letters from sundry parts
of the kingdom have come to my hands, some mentioning strange
sights in the ayre ; others, men fighting therein ; others, guns shooting ;
others, relating of three moons ; others, the apparition of two suns.
Some sending letters, and including therein some part of that corn
which was rained down from heaven. I forbear all further discourse
thereof, assuring the kingdom these prodigies are the premonitors, and
assured infallible messengers of God's wrath against the whole kingdom.—"Astronomical Prediction of the Occurrences in England, 1648,"
by William Lilly, Student in Astrologie. London : 1648.

and of wondrous signs in the heavens. The most
remarkable of these was the appearance for the space
of a whole hour of three suns* at one time in the
sky. These extraordinary apparitions were generally
regarded as heralds and precursors of miseries and
disasters. Nor were the general anticipations of
evil unfulfilled, for, in the early progress of the year,
the greatest of misfortunes befell the nation, in the
sudden resuscitation of a second civil war, to be fiercely
contested by brief, though bloody, struggles in many
quarters of the land.

The King, Charles I., was, at the commencement
of the year 1648, a prisoner at Carisbrook Castle, in
the Isle of Wight, under the custody of Parliament.
The Independents were at this moment the predominant party in the House of Commons, and had begun
to entertain and to publicly avow those designs which
eventually brought their sovereign to a public trial,

---

* Lilly gives, p. 8 of this treatise, an account of these *parhelii*, or
false suns. "Their appearance," he says, "is matutine, or in the morning.
Their motion is always with the sun. They have no heat, are pale, wan,
or dull, and their beams look as if they were of an icey colour. Their
continuance is but short: sometimes they are visible half-an-hour,
sometimes more, seldom longer than one hour. Let us expect from ac-
cidental-suns, rather cold and rains, than heat or lightning; they more
certainly promise rain, and more assuredly than the rods, or streaks, in
the clouds." This is by no means an uncommon phenomenon. At the
battle of Mortimer's Cross, fought Feb. 11, 1460, three suns were seen,
whence Edward IV. assumed the sun triple in full brightness as his
heraldic cognizance.

and an unmerited death. On the 17th day of
January, they induced the House of Commons to
enact a solemn ordinance, refusing henceforth to
enter any treaty or to hold any communication with
their sovereign. The country at large was by no
means prepared to sanction this resolution of the
Parliament. A fervid exuberance of loyal feeling
spread suddenly like an electric shock throughout
the land. The nation, with a movement imposing
by its spontaneous universality, expressed its instinc-
tive dread lest the monarchy should be superseded by
a military despotism, or by a parliamentary usurpa-
tion. In the early spring these general feelings of
discontent and disquietude found expression in divers
simultaneous but ill-organised efforts for the rescue
and restoration of the King. Wales led the way in a
widespread and obstinate rebellion under the gallant
Colonels Poyntz, Poinder, and Powell. Large crowds
assembled in nearly every English county, to show
their sympathy with, and desire for, their sovereign. The freeholders of Surrey thronged the
avenues of Westminster Hall, personally to present
to the Parliament a petition in his favour. The City
of London was for two days in the possession of a
loyal mob. The watchwords of all were, " For God,
the Treaty, and King Charles." So universal was
the reaction, that half the fleet revolted from the

Parliament, and, sailing to the coast of Holland, placed itself at the disposal of, and received as its admiral, the Prince of Wales. Scotland was equally zealous in behalf of its sovereign, and raised an army of 16,000 men, who invaded England under the Duke of Hamilton. A second civil war, in fact, had arisen in the land, and was carried on with such energy, diffusiveness, and determination that its issues were for some time in the balance, so that at the midsummer of this year it was impossible to say whether the termination of the contest would be favourable for Charles I. or for his opponents.

In this position of affairs the town of Colchester became in an unexpected and unlooked-for manner the scene of the most important events connected with this second civil war. The entire county of Essex in the earlier contest with the King, from A.D. 1642 to A.D. 1646, had been among the most devoted adherents of the Parliament, but its inhabitants shared largely on this occasion in the prevailing popular sentiments. The county train-bands summoned to a muster by their commander, Colonel Farre, declared in part for the King; and, choosing Sir Charles Lucas as their general, proceeded to join the Royalist gentry and freeholders of Kent and of the southern counties, who were assembled in arms on Blackheath, to aid in the deliverance of the King. Sir Thomas

Fairfax, sent by the Parliament to effect their dispersion, put them to flight (after an obstinate resistance)
in two successive engagements at Maidstone and at
Rochester.   The defeated but still resolute Royalists
retired across the Thames into Essex, and sought
shelter at Chelmsford ; but, being closely followed by
the army of Fairfax, retreated to Colchester.   Having
reached this town at the end of a long and wearisome
day's march, about six o'clock in the evening of Monday, June 12th, they found the inhabitants to be of
a different spirit to themselves, and favourers of the
Parliament rather than of the King.   A company of
the town train-band was drawn across the London
road to dispute their entrance, and all the gates were
closed by order of the bailiffs.   A brief interview
ensued between the municipal authorities and the
leaders of the Royalists, which resulted in the surrender of the town to their superior forces, on the
condition that all the rights, liberties, and privileges
of the corporation and of the inhabitants should be
secured, and no tax nor subsidy be demanded.   On
the next day, Tuesday, June 13th, about the hour of
noon, Sir Thomas Fairfax appeared in force before the
walls.   In the full expectation that the generals who
had so far beaten a hasty retreat before his army
could offer no serious resistance to his arms, he sent
forward a "drum and trumpeter" to proclaim an offer

of pardon to all, both leaders and men, on their surrender of the town, and to convey this letter to the Lord Goring, Earl of Norwich, the chief person among the Royalists :—

    " MY LORD,

        " I am come hither with the Parliament forces to reduce those under your command to the obedience of the Parliament. If your Lordship and those under you will instantly lay down your arms, there may be a prevention of much blood that is like to be spilt, and the town preserved from plunder and ruin. The evil must lie with you if you refuse.

        " Yr servant,

            " THOMAS FAIRFAX.

" *June* 13*th*, 1648."

Lord Norwich replied to this challenge with the courtesy of a gentleman, and in language in accordance with his position. He told Sir Thomas Fairfax " that if he would lay down his commission, he would move in his behalf with the King, and did make no doubt he should prevail." After these mutual messages no time was lost on either side in idle parley. The Parliamentarians, as yet embued with a contempt for their opponents, and anticipant of an easy victory, were eager for the fray. The

Royalists, determined to wage no childish war, but to
bear themselves like men entrusted with the last
defence of a noble cause, were no less keen for a trial
of their prowess. A fiercely-contested fight, waged
chiefly on the side of the town which faced the
London road, carried on bravely on both sides, by
men contesting every hedgerow and coign of advantage, and fighting hand to hand with push of pike,
was maintained with equal advantage throughout the
heat of that long summer afternoon ; till at last, as
the sun declined, Fairfax, fairly confessing his loss of
the anticipated prize, ordered the retreat to be sounded
throughout his army, and withdrew his soldiers to their
camp on Lexden Heath. Chagrined, defeated, and
smarting under their unaccustomed repulse, the Parliamentary forces set on fire the houses in the suburb
below Head Gate, and exercised further cruelty on the
inhabitants in demanding of them monies which they
did not possess, and in driving them in crowds from
the shelter of their homes. Thus, by a concurrence
of unforeseen and unpremeditated circumstances,
without any volition or intention on the part of the
chief actors in the transactions, by a compulsory
restraint enforced against the choice of the population, the town of Colchester became for a time the
cynosure of a nation's hopes, the ark of refuge for the
English Royalists, and the famous scene of one of

the most remarkable and interesting episodes in the whole range of English history.

The two armies now on the threshold of a fierce and protracted contest were in some points very like, and in others very unlike, each other. They were alike in both being composed of Englishmen, equal in the firmness of their attachment to the standard under which they marched, in the resolute pluck and indomitable native courage by which they asserted their opinions even unto death. They were very unlike in the external and adventitious advantages of their respective circumstances. On the one side was an undisciplined host of about 4,000 men (3,000 foot, and 1,000 horsemen), who had gradually concentrated themselves in one body under their present commanders. The mass of these men were raw country fellows, strangers to each other, collected out of different counties, called together from the plough or flail, under the immediate influence of their squires and landlords, without union, discipline, preparation, training in arms, or military experience. Here were the men of Kent, under Lords Loughborough and Norwich ; of Essex, under Sir George Lisle and Sir Charles Lucas ; of Herts, under Lord Capel ; some few Walloons or Flemings, under Sir Bernard Gascoigne ; with a small fraction of Londoners, and some recruits from the train-bands and militia of the

market towns and counties. This heterogeneous and
motley company, scarcely worthy to be called an
army, without plan, fixed purpose, commissariat, or
materiel, were led by men ignorant for the most part
of the rules and strategy of war, who had previously
lived at home as magistrates and peaceful country
gentlemen. They were exposed, moreover, during
the whole time of their occupation of Colchester to
the enmity of the inhabitants. While Mr. Robert
Buxton, Mr. Lambe, and two or three other members
of the corporation, with Mr. Harman, the chief clergyman in the town, espoused their cause, the great
bulk of the population was hostile* from first to last,
and considerably increased the dangers and difficulties of their position. On the other side was Sir
Thomas Fairfax, at the head of a standing army,
composed, in a great degree, of men for four long
years trained under his own eye, accustomed to act
together, inured to the discipline of war, confident
in the remembered companionship of many a tented

* So hostile was the spirit of the bailiffs and corporation, that they
dismissed (on June 26th, their annual election day) Mr. Buxton
and Mr. Lambe, with other aldermen and town councillors who supported the Royal cause, from their municipal offices, and that even at
the time when their town was occupied by the Royalist forces. The
fact is attested to this day by the court books of the corporation. It
is an instance of forbearance on the one side, and of independence on
the other, which could only occur among Englishmen, and which could
not be paralleled in any other history.

field, the stern yet fiery conquerors of Croppedy
Bridge, Marston Moor, and Naseby. Here were the
"Ironsides" of Cromwell, under his son-in-law Ireton,
and his lieutenant Fleetwood; the bold dragoons of
Edward Whalley; the hardy troopers of Ewers; the
flying squadron of Scroope; the train-bands of the
Tower; and the serried infantry of Barkstead, Ingoldsby, and Needham. Nothing was lacking that
science, experience, or enthusiasm could supply,
abundance of food, ample forage, materials, and ammunition; an experienced, but perhaps too cautious
general, a brilliant and effective staff, a valorous
soldiery, and a friendly population.

The exact number of Fairfax's forces may be estimated with tolerable accuracy. On the remodelling
of the army by the Parliament, A.D. 1644, each troop
of cavalry was raised to the complement of 100
horsemen, and each company of infantry to 130
soldiers. The effective force of each regiment of the
Parliamentarian standing army may be fairly reckoned
at two-thirds of the regulation number. Fairfax had
under his immediate command, while in pursuit of
the Royalists, twenty troops of horse, which, on the
calculation of sixty-six to the troop, would give him
1,320 horse. He had also under his command
twenty-one companies of foot, which, at the same
rate of eighty to a company, would amount to 1,680

men. In addition to these forces of the standing army, four Essex troops of yeomanry-cavalry under Colonel Harlackenden, and two regiments of Essex train-bands under Colonel Cooke and Sir Thomas Honeywood, joined him at Chelmsford. These regiments probably did not muster so strongly as those of the regular army. Their number may be reckoned at fifty for each troop of cavalry and sixty for each company of infantry, which would amount to 1,000 men. Within six days of his reaching Colchester, these forces were further augmented by nine additional troops of cavalry, under Colonels Scroope and Ewers, veteran forces, flushed with the pride of triumph in their late return from a successful campaign in Wales. Besides these reinforcements,* he received very shortly a further accession of strength by the arrival of six regiments of train-bands from

* Estimate of army of Sir Thomas Fairfax :—

CAVALRY—STANDING ARMY.

4 troops	(General's Own Horse), Col. Desborough	264	
6	,, Col. E. Whalley................................	396	
5	,, Colonel Fleetwood	330	
3	,, (Ironsides), Col. Ireton......................	198	
2	,, (Dragoons), Capt. Freeman	132	
3	,, (Flying Squadron), Col. Scroope	198	
6	,, Col. Ewer...	396	
		—	1,914
4 troops of Essex Horse, Col. Harlackenden..............		260	
1 troop of Cambridge Horse, Col. Turner...................		50	
1 regiment of Suffolk Horse, Col. Gordon		400	
	Carry forward.................	—	**2,624**

the counties of Suffolk and Cambridge, with several
squadrons of horse. The sum total of the Parliamentary army must have exceeded 6,000 men of
all arms; and these were supplemented by a large
number of labourers, hired by the day to assist in
forming the ditches, graffes, and entrenchments.
This brief comparison of the forces on either side
will tend to illustrate the marvellous endurance, the
patient industry, the skilful contrivances, the creation
and husbandry of resources by which the weaker and
worst prepared combatants so long baffled and kept
at bay their numerous and more formidable opponents.

INFANTRY—STANDING ARMY.

		Brought forward...............		2,624
10 companies, Col. Barkstead		800		
7 ,,	(Tower regiment), Col. Needham...	560		
4 ,,	Col. Ingoldsby	360		
			— 1,720	
2 regiments of Essex train-bands, Cols. Cooke and Sir Thomas Honeywood...................................		800		
4 Suffolk regiments, under Cols. Bloise, Harvey, Fothergill, and Sir Thomas Barnardiston..................... 1,600				
			—	4,120
		Grand total............		6,744

CHAPTER II.

FROM THE COMMENCEMENT OF THE SIEGE TO THE FIRST INVESTMENT OF THE TOWN.

" Hold out then stiffly, Colchester ! and be
A miracle to all posteritie."

Old Ballad.

Fairfax's council of war—The policy of Fairfax—Topography of
Colchester—The strength of the south side of the town—The first
location of the Parliamentarian army—The state of the town walls
—The fortunate discovery of provisions at the Hyth—The policy of
the Royalists—Commencement of Fort Essex and Royal Fort—An
intercepted letter—Mr. Wigmore's horses—Colonel Ewers joins Fairfax
—Royalist foraging expeditions—First failure of Royalist hopes—Mr.
Owen's sermon—A present for Sir Thomas Fairfax—Unusual wetness
of the season—The first shot fired at the town—Arrival of the Suffolk
forces—Completion of investment—The distance of entrenchments
from the walls.

SIR THOMAS FAIRFAX, the general of the Parliamentarian forces, sorely perplexed at the sudden
alteration in the tide of affairs, and astonished by
the resolute front of his hitherto despised foemen,
summoned on the morrow of his repulse, in the early
dawn of Wednesday, June 14th, his chief officers to
hold in his tent a council of war. The result of their
deliberations was a resolve to obtain by some means or

other possession of the town, even though it should
involve the slow and painful process of a formal
siege.   This resolution of Fairfax and his council
implied a public acknowledgment of their repulse,
and the amplest recognition of the valour and determination of their opponents.   The Parliamentarian
general pursued, however, the most prudent policy,
and adopted the wisest course.   He had now caught,
as in a trap, the chief Royalist leaders, and by retaining
them at Colchester he confined to this one spot the
ablest promoters of the insurrection, preserved other
counties from the danger of its contagion, prevented any
chance of the junction of the English revolters with
their Scotch allies on the eve of invading England
under their general the Duke of Hamilton, and, in a
word, adopted the most effectual method of stamping
out the opposition, and of neutralising the efforts of
the loyal adherents of the King.

The town of Colchester, when thus beleaguered by
the forces of Fairfax, was very different to what it is
now.   Built on a considerable eminence, in the form
of a parallelogram, it was in the year 1648 a complete
and extensive fortification, containing an area of 118
acres, enclosed entirely by lofty and thick walls, made
of brick, stone, and flints by the hands of its early
Roman masters.   These walls were pierced by five chief
entrances, provided with closed gates, and crowned

with turrets, barbicans, and loopholes for musqueteers
and marksmen.   Three of these gateways, Head Gate,
Schire Gate, and St. Botolph's Gate, were placed in the
south wall, and rendered this south side of the town
the most effective for either offensive or defensive
purposes.   This south side of the town was further
strengthened in a remarkable way by an ecclesias-
tical building called St. Botolph's Priory, by the tall
garden walls and embattled gate-house of St. John's
Abbey, and more effectually still by the stately and
extensive mansion of Sir John Lucas, which, though
placed without the walls, was yet near enough to
form, in its quadrangled court-yards, lengthened galleries, and lofty roofs, a separate citadel and fortress
for the protection of the town.   The other two entrances were East Gate and North Gate.   The first of
these was strong by reason of its proximity to a
stream, on which a capacious mill served as an admirable redoubt; and the other, located in the
extreme north end of the west wall, was protected
by the River Colne, which flowed right round the
town close below the walls for the whole distance between the East and the North Gate.   The Royalists
also occupied the Hyth, or the port of Colchester,
about three-quarters of a mile distant from the walls
on the east side of the town, which, with its church
and warehouses, formed a sort of exterior redoubt or

fortress of considerable strength. All the points
mentioned in this brief account of the topography of
the town will recur again in their turn during the
progress of the siege, as the scenes of carnage and
of desperate conflict between the combatants. Fairfax,
however, fully conscious of the greater strength of
the south side of the town, and of it affording the
most convenient facilities of approach, concentrated
at the first on this side the main body of his army.
He placed along this front of the town four troops of
his own regiment, seven troops of Cromwell's "Ironsides" under the command of Colonels Ireton and
Fleetwood, three squadrons of Scroope's, the two
most reliable regiments of foot-guards under Colonels
Barkstead and Ingoldsby, the forces of the county of
Essex, both horse and foot, under Colonels Cooke
and Harlackenden. He entrusted the charge of East
Gate to the experience of Colonel Edward Whalley,
with an injunction to keep a special watch on the
Ipswich and Wyvenhoe roads. The North Gate was
reserved for the custody of Colonel Ewers, whom he
daily expected to join his camp; while the north side,
the most difficult of access by reason of the river below
the walls, was for the present left for the county regiments summoned to join him from Suffolk and from
Cambridgeshire. Such was the first preliminary location of the Parliamentarian forces. Fairfax also, with

the prudence of a practised commander, detached
troops to the Isle of Mersey, as a precaution against
help or supplies being conveyed to the town from the
sea, and broke up the roads with great ditches and
banks to hinder his opponents in any efforts they
might make to escape.

The besieged Royalists quickly discerned the intended strategy of Fairfax, and applied themselves to
meet the exigencies of their perilous position with the
courage pertaining to men who had consented to
jeopardise their lives for a noble cause.   Their first
step was to apportion out among themselves the responsible oversight of the important affairs.   Lord
Norwich* was made the Governor of the town, Lord
Capel Director of the Council of War, Sir Charles
Lucas Commander-in-Chief of the horse, and Sir
George Lisle of the foot.   Lord Loughborough, a

* Sir George Goring was a gentleman of good family in Sussex. He
served in the Low Countries under Sir Francis Vere, and, having distinguished himself, was created Baron Goring in 1632. On the breaking out of the civil war, he was made Governor of Portsmouth, and
took, at a later period, an active part in the war. He commanded a
regiment of cavalry at the battle of Marston Moor, and after that did
the King much service in the West of England. He was created Earl
of Norwich in 1644. At the termination of the war, he joined the
Prince of Wales in Holland, and on the breaking out of the second
civil war returned to England with the commission of Generalissimo of
the Royal forces.   On his reprieve from death, by the casting vote of
Lenthall, the Speaker, he was banished the kingdom.   He returned at
the Restoration, and died, A.D. 1663, at his house at Brentford, Middlesex.

civilian, was entrusted with the control of the commissariat. The next step was a minute examination of the walls, and of all the means at hand to secure an effective resistance. The walls were reported as being co-extensive with the whole circuit of the town, but in many parts miserably out of repair. Only one fort, called the Old Fort, or the Balkon,* situated in the south wall, near St. Mary's Church, was found fit for immediate use. Measures were at once adopted for the speedy formation, at the requisite places, of sconces, ramparts, counterscarps, and platforms. The chief anxiety that troubled the Royalist leaders was the anticipated scarcity of provisions and of gunpowder. They were fortunate, however, to find both these in most unlooked-for quantity.

Colchester at the period of this history was one of the most important commercial towns on the east coast. It not only had a trade of cloths peculiar to itself, of which a subsequent chapter will treat, but it was a place of export for various kinds of grain, and had a harbour and quay, known by the name of the Hyth, close to the walls of the town, and now occupied by the Royalists. It so happened that at this time the merchants of London had laid up in their warehouses at the Hyth a great store of wheat, barley,

* The balkon is a round projecting portion of the wall. It is supposed to be derived from Balke, a beam.

peas, rye, besides large supplies of salt fish, oil, wine,
spice, raisins, starch, and currants, and, what they
valued and needed above all these, a vast quantity of
gunpowder. These unlooked-for resources encouraged
the hopes of the besieged. All was not dark in their
horizon. Regarding their timely discoveries "as a
Providence as great as that of the manna to the
Israelites in the wilderness, for in the memory of
man never had been known such plenty at the Hyth
as there was at that time," they dared to look forward in a spirit of self-reliance to the issues of the
contest enforced on them by Fairfax. "We had
hopes of reliefe" (writes one of their number in this
very moment of incipient strife) "both from the Scots
and from diverse other places; besides it was judged
the greatest piece of policy to keep the enemy, and to
give a remora to their delay, by which we had given
a liberty to others who were then in action to work
their designs without interruption."

The lists being thus set for a long and determined
struggle, the leaders on either side lost no time in
applying themselves respectively to expediting the
attack or consolidating the defence. Fairfax commenced his operations on Thursday, June 15th, ·by
marking out in the fields lying south of the present
London road a large fort to command St. Mary's
Church, the Head Gate, and the south-west corner of

c 2

the walls, and called it, in compliment to the forces of the county, Fort Essex. This fort, containing an area of 20,000 yards, being eight roods in width by three roods in depth, and designed for eight pieces of artillery and for the shelter of 1,000 men, continued throughout the contest to be the very Mamelon of the Parliamentarian position. The besieged, with a watchful jealousy of the doings of their opponents, commenced at once the construction of a platform in the churchyard of St. Mary's, and named it "The Royal Fort," from which they fired on the workmen and soldiers labouring in the preparation of Fort Essex, and caused much mischief to their enemies throughout the siege.

An incident occurred on this day, Thursday, June 15th, which illustrates the state and temper of the times, and exhibits the feelings of neighbours towards each other under the exasperating influences of civil strife. Some of the inhabitants of Manningtree, a small town about eight miles from Colchester, having formed themselves into a committee for the pro-motion of the interests of the Parliament, intercepted a private letter, which they at once forwarded to Gene-ral Fairfax, with the accompanying explanation :—

" May it please your Excellencie,

" We whose names are subscribed, being inhabitants in the town of Manningtree, have inter-

cepted a letter which was sent from Master Robert
Vezey to his wife, and a warrant to the High Con-
stable. We keep the originals, and have sent you a
true copy of them, as is our duty, that yr Excellency
may deale or proceed thereon, as in yr wisdome you
shall think fit, and remain in all humbleness, praying
for yr helth and safety, with good and prosperous
success in God's cause.

" Your humble servants to command,
    " JOSEPH BURWIST.   HENRY HAYES.
    " JOHN MICKLEFIELD.   NICHOLAS WOOLVET.
        " EDMUND CHAUNTRELLER.
" *Manningtree, 15th June,* 1684."

The letter itself will be interesting, as exhibiting
the feelings prevailing in the breasts of the Royalists
at this time.

" DEARE HEART,

      " My love prefixt. My suite to thee is to
further my engagement under Sir Charles Lucas,
General of his Majesty's forces now at Colchester,
with such money and linen as upon the suddaine
may be provided for me, and to send the same to me
to my cosen Buxtones, where I have quartered this two
nights. I earnestly desire thee not to be dismayed,
for we trust in God we shall be able to make good

our cause against the fury of the enemy. I cannot
send thee the particulars of what hath happened
since my coming forth, I being now in haste to send
for my souldiers* that are gone home. The next I
hope shall give thee a full relation. In the mean-
time, committing thee and thine to the protection of
the Almighty, I remaine,

> " Thy loving husband,
>
> " ROBERT VEZEY.

" *Colchester, June* 14*th*, 1648.

" To my very loving wife Mrs. Ann Vezey these
present."

During this early period of the siege Fairfax made
use of the summer evenings, and broke fresh ground
every night, his engineers availing themselves of the
darkness to mark out the lines of their entrenchments, forts, and redoubts. On Friday, June 16th,
he issued this order to his troops, which was probably
designed to prohibit all irregular searching for food
and marauding :—

" I do hereby order that no souldier nor officer do
presume to straggle a mile from the leaguer, or to
stir away from their colours and duty under pain of

---

* This letter contained an order to the soldiers of his company to
join the Royalist forces at Colchester.

being severely proceeded against according to the
articles of war; and all officers are required at least
twice in every twenty-four hours to call over the list
of the souldiers of their respective companies, and to
take notice of all absent without order or leave.

" THOMAS FAIRFAX."

The besieged on Friday, June 16th, adopted vigorous measures for the recruiting their cavalry mounts.
There was in the town at this time a Mr. Wigmore,
who conducted the chief transport to London of the
goods manufactured at Colchester. This person had
a large number of horses employed by him as the
chief carrier of the neighbourhood, and these the
Loyalists took possession of for the service of their
cavalry. On this day the whole Royalist garrison
was called out to pay due funeral honours to Sir
William Campion, a gallant knight who, having been
severely wounded in the first attack made by Fairfax
on the town, had since died of his wounds. The
ceremony was attended by Lord Norwich, Sir Charles
Lucas, Lord Capel, and the other leaders, who, amidst
their labours and excitement, found time to pay the
rightful debt of gratitude and respect to the sufferers
in their cause.

It were possible from the news-books and diurnals
of the period in the British Museum to assign to

every day some particular transaction. It will be
sufficient to give only a brief epitome of the chief
events which preceded and led to the first investment of the town.

On Sunday, June 18th, Colonel Ewers joined the
Parliamentarian camp. He brought with him six
companies of horse, just set at liberty by the successful attack on Chepstow Castle, in Monmouthshire,
and was immediately located at the north-west corner
of the town, with a charge to watch the north Gate,
and to hinder the besieged from any attempt to col-
lect forage or to escape in that direction. The
Royalists kept up during this day a brisk cannonade,
more especially directed against the working parties
employed in the construction of Mount Essex. At
nightfall they made a good use of the horses of Mr.
Wigmore, lately pressed into their service, for planning
a sortie in force out of East Gate, as yet very im-
perfectly watched; they brought in a large convoy of
sheep, oxen, and provisions, from Tendring Hundred,
though Sir Charles Lucas, with an unprecedented
and scarcely justifiable generosity, forbade anything
to be taken from the lands of those known to be
favourable to the King. The saddest penalties of
war fell with an equal hand on all its votaries.
Neither combatant can claim exemption in a game so
prodigal of life; and as the Royalists had just paid

the last sad offices of respect to one of their leaders,
so on this day Sir Thomas Fairfax and his staff conveyed with all honour to a soldier's sepulchre the
remains of a gallant companion in arms, Colonel
Needham, the commander of the London train-bands,
who had died from wounds received in the unsuccessful attempt upon the town. The deaths of these
two generals attest the severity of that first combat,
and the strenuous efforts made by Sir Thomas Fairfax
for the successful accomplishment of his wishes.

In the middle of this week, about Wednesday,
June 21st, various tidings of evil import reach the
Royalist leaders. The Suffolk forces were announced
as having mustered at Nayland, on the bank of the
Stour, the boundary of the county, and of having
entertained scruples about marching out of their own
shire. Lord Norwich on this sent to them gentlemen of influence, to induce them to join him. His
negotiations proved entirely unavailing, and at the end
of the week, on the following Saturday, June 24th,
the Suffolk train-bands, consisting of four regiments
of foot under Colonels Bloise, Harvey, Fothergill, and
Sir Thomas Barnardiston, and numbering a thousand
men exactly, joined the Parliamentarian army. Sir
Thomas Fairfax placed them at once on the north
side of the town, and enjoined on them the special
duty of watching the East and North Gates. Nor was

this the only event of the week disastrous to the
Royalists. A gallant officer, Major Muscamp, who
had raised some soldiers, and was marching to the
relief of the garrison in Colchester and to the attack
of Fairfax, was suddenly challenged and defeated by
troops despatched from the Parliamentarian camp.
This was the first failure in the hopes entertained by
the Royalists that their friends without the town
would exert themselves and effect their deliverance;
but it was an over-true forerunner of all such efforts,
not one of which was attended with success. Captain
Robert Vezey, too, the writer of the letter already
quoted, was during this week taken prisoner, not
without some suspicion of having been a willing party
to his own capture. Four Walloon soldiers, also, ex-
traordinarily well mounted, and as well armed with
blunderbuss pistols, each of which would carry seven
bullets, were intercepted and conveyed as prisoners to
Fairfax's head-quarters. These instances of evil
fortune were only compensated by two incidents
favourable to the Royalists. They made during the
week some more successful forays at night into the
district of the Tythering Hundred, and also secured
one important step in advance of their opponents by
turning Sir John Lucas's well-built mansion into a
fortress, and by occupying it with a select band of a
hundred picked soldiers.

An incident worth mentioning is recorded of Sunday, June 25th. On that day Mr. Owen,* the Puritan pastor of the church at Coggeshall, preached at the head-quarters before the Lord General. There is no record of his sermon beyond this one sentence : he said, " Fire and faggots are no good reformers."

On the next day, Monday, June 26th, the town of Chelmsford sent a present to Sir Thomas Fairfax—two kegs of sturgeons, two kegs of fresh salmon, venison, twelve dozen pullets, a great store of fowls, vessels of wine, and a large quantity of vinegar and salt.

The periodicals of the day abound at this crisis of the siege with complaints of the extreme wetness and inclemency of the season. The prodigies which

* The Rev. John Owen, the son of an English clergyman, was born at his father's vicarage, Stadham, in Oxfordshire, A.D. 1616. Admitted as a student at Queen's College, Oxford, after taking his degree he became an Independent minister, and obtained from the Parliament the rectory of Coggeshall, Essex. During the siege of Colchester he was more than once requested to preach before Fairfax and his army. So great was his zeal for the Parliament that, after other ministers had declined, he preached a sermon before the House of Commons on the very day after the execution of King Charles I. Cromwell was so pleased with him that he made him his chaplain, and, in A.D. 1651, appointed him Dean of Christ Church, and Vice-Chancellor, under himself, of the University of Oxford, on which occasion he received the degree of D.D. Dr. Owen was one of the most learned of the Nonconformist ministers. At the Restoration he was deprived of his offices at the University, and became the minister of a congregation of Independents, meeting for worship in a chapel in Leadenhall Street, London. He died in retirement at Ealing, A.D. 1683.

ushered in the year too truly pourtrayed a heritage
of woe. Whitelock, the chronicler of the passing
events of the day, says of this month of June, without
any reference to the circumstances of this siege :—

"The weather was strangely cold and rainy for this
time of year."

A news-book contains this record :—

"Notwithstanding the unseasonable weather, yet
the soldiers work day and night at several places."

A Royalist narrator sees the hand of a Divine
visitation in the unusual inclemency of the season :—

" How have the heavens seemed to fight against
them since they besieged that despised place (Colchester), for indeede, tho' the judgment of rain
hath been upon us all, and threatens a general
calamity to every one (which, indeede, we have all
deserved); yet it cannot be denyed that they have
been most specially detrimental in their designe, by
those bottles of heaven which God hath poured out
upon them in their trenches, whereby their soldiers
are much impaired in their health."

In spite, however, of these obstacles and difficulties,
the perseverance of Fairfax and the spirit of his
engineers made a marked progress in their purposed
investment of the town. Besides their labours on
Fort Essex they had successfully completed one fort
(mounted with two cannon) at the north-west corner

of the entrenchments for the purpose of annoying the
defenders of the North Gate. Fort Ingoldsby (as it
was called, after the colonel whose forces guarded
that point) discharged on the very day of the arrival
of the Suffolk forces the first fire of artillery directed
against the walls. At the same time a military bridge
was constructed across the River Colne, in the close
vicinity of North Gate, and thus a more easy passage
and more intimate communication was established
between the troops located on either side of the
Colne. There was only one more step wanted, and
that was the effectual strengthening of the leaguer at
the East Gate, so that the foraging parties, hitherto
conducted so successfully by that outlet, should be
stopped. To effect this the Tower regiment was
ordered to encamp near the East Gate, to assist the
Suffolk train-bands in their task of hemming in their
foes on that side of the town.

Thus the first investment was completed at the
expiration of a fortnight by the location of the forces
of Fairfax around the entire circuit of the walls. The
main body of the Parliamentary veterans held the
south side, Colonel Ingoldsby's experienced battalions
the west, the Suffolk train-bands the north, while the
east was committed to the keeping of the train-bands of
the Tower. The whole circumvallation of these military
lines is said to have exceeded ten miles in length.

Such extensive camp-works were never seen in England before or since. They were, however, placed for the most part, especially on the south side, at a considerable distance from the walls, in some portions as far off as one or two miles. The space, therefore, between the town and the entrenchments provided an ample battle-field, and an abundance of room for sorties, sallies, and conflicts, for fight or flight, for manœuvres of either cavalry or infantry, and for every kind of military encounter. The narration of some of these fiercely-contested engagements will form the subject of the fifth chapter of this history.

CHAPTER III.

THE IMPRISONMENT AND RELEASE OF SIR WILLIAM MASHAM.

> " No radiant pearl, which crested Fortune wears,
> No gem, that tinkling hangs from Beauty's ears ;
> Nor the bright stars, which Night's blue arch adorn,
> Nor rising sun that gilds the vernal Morn ;
> Shine with such lustre as the Tear that flows
> Down Virtue's manly cheek for others' woes."
>
> WALTER SCOTT.

Exasperation of the times—Seizure of Sir William Masham—Exertions of the Parliament on his behalf—Letter of inquiry about his welfare—A military execution—An account of the fellow-prisoners of Sir William Masham—Their mediation for a treaty—Reply of Sir Thomas Fairfax and of Lord Norwich—Proposal to exchange the son of Lord Capel for Sir William Masham—Lord Capel's answer—Sir William Masham exchanged for Mr. John Ashburnham—Indulgences granted to, and care taken of, the fellow-prisoners of Sir William Masham.

IT is difficult in the well-ordered events of a settled government to realise the total disruption of the ordinary classes of society and the painful separation of friend from friend entailed on a land under the exasperations of civil warfare. This short chapter will give, not only in the episode of the history of Sir William Masham, but in the other facts recorded in it, a practical illustration and example of the dealings of English gentlemen with their own fellow-countrymen when arrayed on different sides of the great political controversy of the 17th century.

The Royalists in their hasty flight through Chelmsford surprised and captured a number of country gentlemen connected with the county of Essex, whom they found sitting as a committee for furthering the interests of the Parliament, and whom they retained in a strict but honourable captivity at Colchester. The chief and most eminent person among these detained prisoners was Sir William Masham, a representative of the county, a member of the Westminster Assembly of Divines, and a popular man in the House of Commons. His colleagues in Parliament were indignant at his capture, and exerted themselves to the utmost to effect his deliverance. For this purpose the House of Commons, on Thursday, June 15th, within three days of the commencement of the siege, ordered "that twenty Royalist delinquents should be sent to General Sir Thomas Fairfax, to be dealt with by him according as the Parliamentary Commissioners were treated" in the town of Colchester.

They did more than this. With a zeal for their friends which met with almost universal reprobation they sent a band of soldiers to Hadham Hall, the country seat of Lord Capel, in Hertfordshire, and took forcible possession of his eldest son, a youth of sixteen years, and conveyed him to Fairfax's camp, as an additional hostage for the safety of the committee.   On these proceedings being reported to Fairfax, he sent a trumpeter to Sir Charles Lucas, the Commander-in-Chief of the forces in the town, with this letter :—

"Sir,

"I understand you have in custody Sir Wm. Masham, a Parliament man, and some other gentlemen prisoners.   I desire you to permit this bearer to see in what condition they are, what necessaries they want, that care may be taken for supplying them.   I have about 500 prisoners of yours.   If you have any of my soldiers prisoners, I desire to know the number and quality of them, and shall send as many in exchange ; which shall be performed by me,

"Thomas Fairfax.

"17 *of June*."

The officer accompanying the trumpet was allowed the requested interview ; and this answer was sent in reply to the proposed exchange of prisoners of war :—

"My Lord,

"I desire you will by the trumpeter send up a list of all those gentlemen officers and souldiers of

our party and under our command that are now
prisoners in your army. We shall upon the like
occasion show the same respect to you; and we
desire the trumpeter may speak with the best quality
of our prisoners, to let them know our endeavour
for their enlargement. Wee have detained yr
trumpeter longer by reason of our hourly motion
and action.

"My Lord, wee rest

"Your servants,

"NORWICH. LOUGHBOROUGH.

"ARTHUR CAPEL. CHARLES LUCAS.

"17 *June*, 1648.

"My Lord, we do also hereby return you many
thanks for yr honourable civilities in the business of
Sir Wm. Layton."

This mutual desire for the interchange of prisoners
was never carried out. The list returned by Fairfax
contained the names of so many men of whom
Lord Norwich and his friends had no knowledge,
that they were compelled to decline the proposal for an
exchange. On this refusal being clearly ascertained,
General Fairfax called a council of his officers, to
discuss what was to be done with the prisoners.
The result of the discussion was an order "that
every fifteenth man of the Essex forces being a
batchelor, and every tenth man being married, and

every fifth man of the Londoners and Kentish forces, should be shot; and that all the rest being batchelors should be sent beyond the seas, and the married men to their families."

This cruel military execution was carried out in Fairfax's camp on the morning of Monday, June 19th, when the prisoners cast lots to decide their fate, and when the rescued married men were dismissed on parole to their homes. This painful fact, so ominous of the evil influence even on the noblest natures effected by the fiend of civil strife, is recorded alike by the Parliamentarian and Royalist chroniclers. The testimony of both friend and foe attests the authentication of the narrative.

The postscript of the above letter refers to a happier incident, and bears witness to the courtesy of Fairfax. Sir William Layton was a Royalist. He had been wounded in the foot by a bullet in the first attack by Fairfax on the town, and had been conveyed as a prisoner to the camp of the General on Lexden Heath. He was a civilian, and not a soldier ; and this fact may perhaps account in part for the kindly care he had received at the hands of Fairfax, and for which the thanks of the Royalist leaders are expressed in the postscript of their letter.

Sir William Masham and the other gentlemen of the county of Essex at this time detained by the

Royalist defenders of Colchester occupied a very peculiar position. They were all persons of consequence by their wealth, family connections, and territorial possessions. Their political and personal sympathies were avowedly with the besiegers, and yet, as prisoners to the besieged, they were desirous as far as possible to further their wishes; so that by their position they became as it were by mutual consent the mediators between the combatants, and stood out on various occasions as prominent characters in the solemn drama that was being enacted. At an early period of the siege they volunteered their services, in the hope of preventing the impending conflict, and of obtaining a treaty between the leaders of the forces now brought face to face to each other in the field.

The following letters give an account of the proceeding :—

" *To the Lord Fairfax.*

"My Lord,

"We have sent the enclosed to yr perusall, and shall need say no more than what the enclosed speaks.

"We rest, your servants,

"Norwich. Arthur Capel.
"Charles Lucas."

" *Enclosure.*

" The Committee of Parliament now under restraint at Colchester, upon their humble request for it to the Lord Norwich, Lord Capel, and Sir Charles Lucas, have obtained leave of them that they, the said Committee, may make it their humble proposall to Lord Fairfax that there may be a treaty betwene both armies for a peace.

" W. ROWE.	W. MASHAM.
" IS. EEDON.	ROBERT EVANS.
" SAMUEL SHEFFIELD.	J. LANGLEY.
" J. MIDDLETON.	THOS. AYLOFF.
" ROBERT SMITH.	L. BARNARDISTON.

" It is the general peace of the kingdome we contend for, and therefore we are content that the Committee shall send this above-written proposall to the Lord Fairfax, according unto their request made to us.

" NORWICH.   ARTH. CAPEL.
" CHARLES LUCAS.

" *For my Lord Fairfax.*
    " *June* 19*th*, 1648."

Sir Thomas Fairfax returned an answer both to the Committee and to the Royalist leaders.   He

refused to accede to the proposal for a treaty between
the armies, and repeated the terms of his original
demand for an unconditional surrender of the town,
with the promise of the lives of all, and of a
permission to all to return in safety without hurt
or molestation to their homes. This correspondence
terminated with a second letter from the Royalist
leaders to Fairfax :—

"My Lord,

"The conditions you proffer to the officers
and soldiers on our part we do hereby offer to the
officers and souldiers on your part. We shall on this
occasion deal plainly. We do not without evident
reason conceive ourselves to be in a condition to
resist all the force you can make, and thereby to
give courage and opportunity to all true-hearted
Englishmen to recover their antient and knowne
lawes ; or if you should adventure to attaque us, we
doubt not, by the mercy and assistance of Almighty
God, to give you such a repulse as shall give testimony
of our force and courage, and at how high a rate
we value the general peace of the kingdome.

"Norwich.   Charles Lucas.
"*June* 20*th*, 1648."

Although this effort of the Essex Committee to

promote a truce between the combatants proved
abortive, yet Fairfax, perpetually importuned by frequent communications from the House of Commons,
endeavoured by every inducement he could think of
to obtain from the Royalist leaders the release of the
members of the Committee. They were, however,
reluctant to give them up, in the expectation (an
expectation by no means justified by the result)
that their retention to the last would prove an
influential element in obtaining for themselves, in
the event of their defeat, more favourable terms, and
an exemption from a fatal sentence, as the penalty
of their daring.

Fairfax, however, laboured most to secure the
deliverance of Sir William Masham. On Friday,
June 30th, he sent a trumpeter to make a direct
proposal to exchange him for the youthful son of
Lord Capel. It must have been a grievous trial
and exquisite pain to Lord Capel, but to such a
patriot there could be but one answer. He remon-
strated with Sir Thomas Fairfax on the inhumanity
of the Parliament in forcibly seizing his son, who
was not in arms against them, and protested against
the act as unsanctioned by the rules and practices of
all honourable warfare ; but he further said " that he
joyed to see any of his, if in no other way, yet by his
suffering to pay the duty they owe to the King and

to the known laws of the kingdom," and indignantly refused the proposal.

At last, after many negotiations, an arrangement satisfactory to both parties was effected. Mr. John Ashburnham, the chief aider and abettor of the King in his escape from Hampton Court, who had incurred the extreme displeasure of the Parliament, was proposed and accepted in exchange for the popular representative, and Sir William Masham left Colchester a free man on Sunday, the 30th of July. Those, however, must have been strange times when neighbour was thus pitted against neighbour, and fellow-countrymen weighed against fellow-countrymen. The other gentlemen of the county, members of the Committee, were retained as prisoners throughout the whole duration of the siege. They received, however, during their involuntary sojourn with their Royalist foes every possible attention. As the perils of the siege increased, they were carefully removed out of the risk of danger. By the extended courtesy of their jailers, when the later severer privations of the siege began, they were allowed to receive daily from the quarters of Fairfax the best of provisions and the richest viands, venison pasties, hot joints, delicate jellies. They will again be heard of at the end of the siege, taking part in important negotiations between the combatants.

CHAPTER IV.

A WORD ABOUT THE "BAYS" AND "SAYS" MAKERS.

> " All in a kirtle of discoloured say
> lle clothed was."
>
> SPENSER.

The introduction of the "Bays" and "Says" into Colchester—The description of "Bays" and "Says"—A singular importation of foreigners—Their numbers and distribution in the town—Their influence on the "Bays" and "Says" trade—Petition of "Bays" and "Says" makers to Fairfax—His proposal to purchase their goods—The failure of the negotiations—Extinction of "Bays" and "Says" trade.

THE town of Colchester from an early period was remarkable for the manufacture of a particular kind of woollen cloths, known as "Bays" and "Says." The first introduction of this trade into the town can be distinctly traced to the Flemish artisans who came into England from the Low Countries at the especial invitation, and under the fostering care, of the far-sighted and enterprising sovereign Edward IV. The records of the corporation for this period, yet extant, contain the rules and bye-laws of this fellowship, " with the oaths administered by the bailiffs to the officers appointed to weigh and measure the cloths, called Bays and Says ; " and thus prove the establishment of this trade, and the extensive demand for these cloths.*

The same authentic sources of information relate a more modern, and a not less important accession of foreign cloth-makers. The municipal documents con-

---

* It is generally agreed that the "Bays" were a woollen cloth with a long nap. There is a greater difference of opinion about the "Says." Archdeacon Nares, in his glossary, gives a (not admissible) derivation from the French word *soie*, silk. The fabrics with which this word is associated in the demagogue Jack Cade's insulting speech to Lord Say and Seale, implies that it is a less worthy material than silk—

> "Thou say, thou serge, thou buckram lord."
> "HENRY VI.," Act iv., s. 7.

Spenser, too, in the "Faery Queen," uses the word as denoting an article different from silk—

> "His garment neither was of silke nor say."
> Book III., Canto vii., line 3.

. And again he mentions the word in Book I., Canto ii., line 3—

> "All in a kirtle of discoloured say
> He clothed was."

Others derive the word from the Latin *Sagum*, the smart short military cloak worn by the Roman soldiers, and made of Say. "Belli insignem amictum armis militum humerisque superinjectum."—Valer. Andreas. Dissert. de Toga et Sago, p. 11 : Coloniæ, 1618. Whatever he the precise derivation, the "Say" was most probably a woollen cloth, very similar to the "Bays," but of a somewhat inferior texture. A tradition prevails that the "Says" were largely exported from Colchester to Spain, for the cloaks of the muleteers and the Spanish soldiery. The suitableness of "Say" for military cloaks (and silk would be useless for the purpose) may account for the willingness of Fairfax to purchase them for the use of his soldiers.

"Minshen's Dict." 1617, says, a kind of serge made of wool.

tain a long list of "strangers, menne, women, and
children within the towne. The xxvi daie of Aprile,
1573, in the tyme of Robert Lambe and Thomas
Laurence, bailiffs, which fled out of the countrie of
Flanders for conscience sake, by reason of the tyran-
ous usage of the Papistes there, and permitted to
remaine in Colchester by license from the Quene's
Majestie Privie Counsell." These strangers came
with their servants and children, and formed a little
colony of themselves. They amounted to 491 persons, viz., 23 servants, 200 children, and 268 men
with their wives. They were distributed by the
authorities in eighty different houses in all parts of
the town. In addition to these emigrants from
Flanders there were ten French families, whose names
and residences are also given in this list. These
French strangers had four servants and 19 children ;
so that the whole importation of foreigners at this
time amounted to 534 souls. These refugees from
the persecutions of Philip II. of Spain, and from the
cruelties of his general, the Duke of Alva, gave by
their industrious habits, and their skilful manipula-
tions, a great impulse to the cloth trade, so that at
the time of the famous siege of Colchester a large
part of the population of the town obtained their
livelihood by the making of " Bays " and " Says."
The merchant manufacturers of these fabrics, the

descendants of these foreigners, were much affected by
their town being suddenly and unexpectedly made
the arena of a protracted and sanguinary warfare.
Having obtained the approval and co-operation of the
mayor and aldermen, they exerted themselves to obtain
the mutual consent of the Royalist leaders and of
the Parliamentary general to such a relaxation of the
investment as should enable them to carry on the
weekly conveyance of their goods to London. They
presented on Wednesday, June 21st, the following
petition to Lord Norwich, and his council of
officers : —

"The humble petition of the Bay and Say makers
of Colchester. Showeth,—

"That your petitioners having formerly employed
thousands of poor people in this town, in making
Bays and Says, which they have weekly vended at
London ; for this three weeks past the passage thither
being embarred, they are now no longer in any wayes
enabled for the continuancy of the same, except they
may have a license from your Honors, and from the
Lord Generall, the Lord Fairfax, to convey their said
manufactures to the said city of London

"Your petitioners, therefore, humbly pray that they
may have a free passage from your Honors, to convey their Bayes and Sayes, and perpetuanies to Lon-

don by waggons, and that your Honors would be
pleased to recommend their humble duties to the
Lord General Fairfax for the like free passage, with
convoy through his quarters.

"And your petitioners shall humbly pray."

Lord Norwich acceded to the request of the merchants, and sent their petition, accompanied with
another from the mayor, to the General of the Parliamentarian army. Sir Thomas Fairfax refused the prayer
of the petition, "as a thing unheard of in a besieged
town," but stated in his reply, "that he has in his
camp some gentlemen of quality, and townsmen of good
estate and eminent in trade, who offered to buy all
the Bays and Says in the town at a good price, and
to pay for them within a fortnight of the town being
surrendered, and though it were without example in a
besieged town, yet he would give leave, and a safe
convoy for goods and men to any place appointed."

These offers of Fairfax led to no successful negotiations. The purposed free market was never established. The Bays and Says makers were not only
compelled to bear their portion of the present calamity,
but were condemned to feel the severe hand of the
conqueror, and to share in the penalties imposed upon
the town at its surrender, of which they will be found
to pay a full proportion.

The trade of the Bays and Says makers is now extinct. The tradition prevails that it gradually declined from the time of the Peace of Utrecht, 1714, and that in the middle of the 18th century the chief manufacturers finally left Colchester, and settled in the counties of Gloucester and Somerset, where their descendants still carry on a branch of their ancient art in the making of blankets, flannels, and other West of England cloths.

CHAPTER V.

" The death shot hissing from afar,
The shock, the shout, the groan of war."
BYRON.

THE investment of the town of Colchester was a
great blow and discouragement to the besieged. It
changed the whole aspect of their affairs. They
had hitherto been enabled with comparative impunity
to gain access to the country districts adjoining
the East Gate, and to obtain forage and supplies.

They now lost this advantage, and were circumscribed
and hemmed in to the actual circuit of the town.
Every gate was strictly watched and guarded, and no
foraging expedition could be undertaken except at the
risk of a battle. In the meanwhile the entrenchments of Fairfax were being advanced nearer to the
walls, and his forts armed with heavier siege ordnance, forwarded from London. One source of hope
alone remained to the Royalists, the expectation of
relief from without. They trusted that the promised
rising of the Duke of Buckingham and of Lord
Holland, or the general discontent of the great bulk
of the people, or the possible approach of the revolted
fleet, and, above all, that the daily expected invasion
of the Scottish army, under Sir Marmaduke Langdale
and the Duke of Hamilton, might compel Fairfax to
withdraw his army and to raise the siege. In the
meanwhile they did all that men could do. They
abated no jot of heart or hope, and found an antidote
against external fears and internal dissensions in
constant employment, and in the ever present sense
of danger, which of itself brings a charm to brave
men conscious of a noble and disinterested warfare.

The feelings of the Royalists were at this particular
crisis particularly embittered against the newly-ar-
rived Suffolk troops. They had hoped that they
would have come as allies rather than as antagonists,

and the disappointment was hard to bear ; but when, on their arrival, they found that they were encamped in close proximity to the East Gate, and zealously kept them from any nocturnal foraging expedition, their anger was the more enkindled from a sense of injuries rendered by hands that ought to have been friendly. A special and particular animosity arose between them, and the Royalists day by day made sudden attacks on their encampment, annoyed their sentinels, interrupted their workmen, and charged their entrenchments. Not content with these desultory onsets, they resolved to make an organised and combined effort to drive away these forces, and so open out a safe means of gaining access to the country on the east side of the town. At about eight o'clock in the morning of Wednesday, July 5th, about 600 infantry, led by Sir George Lisle himself, and 400 horse, under the immediate command of Sir Charles Lucas, issued out with much speed and gallantry from the East Gate. Their first onset was entirely successful. Their Suffolk foemen fled before them in panic and confusion. They seized without resistance the water-mill at the East Bridge (at a short distance from the East Gate), occupied as their mainguard by the Suffolk auxiliaries, possessed themselves of two guns located there as a battery, and took Captain Moody and his company occupying the

E

redoubt prisoners. A party of the Royalist foot soldiers especially distinguished themselves. They passed in single file, in face of the enemy, over a narrow foot-bridge across the river, within five feet of the enemy's "barricado, as if it had only been a sporting skirmish amongst soldiers at a general muster." The main body of horse and foot proceeded at once over East Bridge, and, by the suddenness and vigour of their attack, repulsed the Parliamentarians on every side. But having pursued the routed forces too far, " more out of heat of courage than of maturer policy," and having exhausted their ammunition, they were obliged to retreat. Colonel Whalley, in charge of that side of the East Gate nearest the Hyth, having seen the dispersion of his Suffolk allies, exerted himself to the utmost in bringing up his soldiers of the standing Parliamentarian army, both horse and foot, and boldly placed himself between the Royalists and the town, so that they had to fight their own way back under the most disadvantageous circumstances. The result was that the Royalists lost all that they had gained. They left behind them the guns captured in their advance, relinquished the mill and guard-house, and lost many prisoners. There was in this battle (for it is more properly described as a battle than a sortie or a skirmish) much hard fighting on both sides. Sir

George Lisle himself was at one time a prisoner, but was speedily rescued by the exertions of his soldiers. In one single spot twenty Royalists were slain, "mostly gentlemen; they could be none else, from their white skins and goodly apparel."

An incident is recorded in connection with this fight which shows the material of which the Royalist army was composed. It is specially related by the news-books of the day, that among those taken prisoners by Whalley's forces was Mr. Weston, who, although the son of a country baronet, Sir Richard Weston, only served as a trooper in the regiment of Sir Charles Lucas. The Parliamentarian loss was severe. Colonel Shambrooke, the successor to General Needham, was slain at the head of the Tower regiment. The Parliamentarians behaved with much cruelty. They are reported to have cut off the hands of the gentlemen before they were dead for the sake of their rings,* and of striking and maiming the prisoners after they were admitted to quarter. They defended this conduct under the erroneous impression that the Royalists had fired with poisoned bullets. Sir Thomas Fairfax, indeed, made at the close of

* The author mentions this statement, as he finds it recorded alike in the *Parliamentarian*, no less than the Royalist, news-books. A journal in the interest of the Parliament narrates, "The colonel, or person of quality, had rings on his fingers, which the soldiers cut off before he was dead."

this conflict a formal complaint upon this point to
Lord Norwich. He and the allied commanders, Sir
Charles Lucas and Sir George Lisle, very indignantly denied and repudiated the imputation, although they confessed " that as for the use of rough
bullets they deny not the practice, and excused themselves, alleging that they were the best they could
send on the sudden."

The Royalists soon began to experience the evil
results of the ·late failure of their bold attempt to
issue from the East Gate and to obtain supplies.
Symptoms of the coming scarcity and suffering were
already apparent. The horses were the first to feel
the biting pressure of short commons. The hay was
all eaten, and the only substitutes were the branches
of trees and the thatch of the houses, which were
unroofed to supply them with the needed nourish-
ment. The townspeople were better provided for. The
council of war had husbanded with the utmost care
all the rich treasures of grain and victualling stores
so fortunately discovered at the Hyth, and now commenced a· distribution of food to the families in the
town. Their first donation amounted to 300 quarters
of wheat and rye. Lord Loughborough undertook
to superintend the allotment of these provisions to
the soldiers and inhabitants, and so great was his
diligence and devotion to his responsible office, that
he is related to have many times spent half-a-day

together, with his strict eye on both millers and bakers, lest by their indirect or wilful neglect any inconvenience should happen.

The rumours of this incipient scarcity were not long in reaching the ears of the Parliamentarian Commander-in-Chief, and, mindful of the interest of his masters in the House of Commons in the members of their Essex Committee, the involuntary prisoners in the hands of the Royalists, he at once sent a trumpeter to Lord Norwich, with the request that he might be allowed to forward provisions for the use of Sir William Masham and his friends. His petition was acceded to, and Lord Norwich desired him to state " at what time, and by what gate, the provisions should be sent," and promised that, " when sent, they should be carefully conveyed to the prisoners." Sir Charles Lucas availed himself of this same opportunity to request Fairfax's " favour to Mr. Weston, that his wounds might be carefully drest, and that he might want no accommodation." It is pleasant to state these instances of mutual civility and forbearance practised towards each other by fellow-countrymen and gallant soldiers in the midst of such an internecine strife. General Fairfax, however, did not extend his courtesy beyond the circle of his own immediate friends and partisans. Some of the ladies of Colchester, impatient of the weariness of the siege, and emboldened, probably, by the interchange of these courtesies between the respective commanders, determined to make the attempt to pass through his encampment to their friends in the country. The incident is thus related : "Mrs. Buxton and Mrs. Lambe, the wives of two Royalist aldermen, with some other ladies, ride boldly out of the town through Fairfax's quarters, but are sent back again into the town. One lady alone, the wife of one known to be well affected to the Parliament, is allowed to pass."

Sir Thomas Fairfax, though he could prohibit all egress from the town without his leave, was not able to prohibit all access to it, nor to prevent the besiegers from holding communication with their friends. On Tuesday, the 4th of July, the very day before the great struggle at the East Gate, "a carrier in disguise, from the Bull Inn, Gracechurch Street, managed to get into the town, and brought word to the Royalist commanders of the rising of the Duke of Buckingham and Earl Holland in behalf of the King, and assured the Royalists, if they would maintain the town a fortnight longer, they would have assistance." This man was one of Mr. Wigmore's carters, and his master vouched to Lord Norwich for his integrity and fidelity, and for the truth and honesty of his communications.

A month had now passed since the army of Fairfax had first appeared before the town of Colchester. The Independents, the predominant party in the

House of Commons, unaccustomed to such resolute
resistance to their commands, and in some measure
suspicious of Fairfax,* determined to send the members of their Committee entrusted with the charge and
direction of the army to visit the headquarters of
their Commander-in-Chief, and to stir him up to
greater exertions. They arrived at the camp on
Saturday, July 8th, and were received with military
honours. They brought with them, as the ostensible
excuse for their visit, an order of the House of
Commons for the trial by court-martial of Captain
Robert Vezey, whose capture has been already related. The council was held in the afternoon of
Saturday, the day of the Commissioners' arrival, and
passed the severe sentence of death upon the prisoner ; but on the solicitation of former friends and
colleagues in the Parliamentary army, and at the
earnest personal entreaty of his wife, Fairfax granted
him a reprieve, and eventually remitted his sentence.

* The visit of the Commissioners indicated the suspicions of the
Parliament. Colonel Ludlow was one of the Commissioners, and he
says that he visited Fairfax in the hope of persuading him to put an
end to the treaty then in progress with the King, but "that he found
him ill-disposed to assist." (Memoirs of Edward Ludlow, Esq. Vivay,
1698, vol. i., p. 262, and see p. 147.) Fairfax himself states in his
Memoirs, " I say, from the time they declared their usurped authority
at Triplot Heath (May, 1646), I never gave my free consent to anything
they did." In a word, Fairfax was known to be lukewarm in his attachment to the Parliament, and was for some months the subject of their
suspicion.

" Whereas Captain Robert Vezey, according to an order of the House of Commons, hath been tryed before my court-martiall, and it hath been resolved that the said Captain is guilty within the first article of the lawes and ordinances of war, of duties in general, for practising and entertaining intelligence with the enemy, and having communications with them, without my directions, and judgment of death having been thereupon given. Now, forasmuch as several gent. of the principall officers of the train-bands for the county of Essex have made their applications unto me, on behalfe of the said Captaine, for pardon of his life, informing, that heretofore he hath been faithfull unto the Parliament, and that they doe believe that the disservice done by him, contrary to the said articles, was out of slavish fear, being prisoner to the enemy, and the said Captain by petition protesting the same, and having entered in an ingagement never to beare arms against the Parliament, or the forces called by their authority, or be assisting thereunto : for these and other reasons of compassion me moving, I do hereby freely remitt and pardon the said Captain Robert Vezey for ever of the execution of the said judgment.

" Given under my hand and seale, at the leaguer before Colchester, this 9th of July, 1648.

" THO. FAIRFAX."

The visit of these Parliamentary Commissioners marked an important era in the proceedings of the siege. If, as it is supposed, their real purpose was to impart new confidence to the councils of Fairfax, and to urge a more vigorous course of action than he had as yet pursued, they effectually succeeded in the object of their coming ; for at this time his attacks upon the enemy were bolder, more systematic, and more continuous than they had hitherto been, although the pluck, courage, and persevering endurance of his antagonists were yet for three long months to withhold from him the prize. Fairfax proceeded at once, under the immediate instigation of these Commissioners, to press forward his advance on the two most important sides of the town. He determined to make an effort on the south-east of the town, to wrest from the Royalists the possession of the Hyth, with its warehouses and its church ; and also to secure, on the south side of the town, the possession of the two important outposts, the mansion of Sir John Lucas and the Gate-house of St. John's Abbey, both of which, with their walled gardens, elevated roofs, and efficient shelter, formed strong defensible positions, held by the Royalists to the exceeding annoyance of their enemies, and to their own very great advantage. He entrusted the conduct of the first of these attacks to his experienced and impetuous colleague, Colonel Whalley, and reserved the second for his own immediate superintendence.

The success of Colonel Whalley in the expedition thus entrusted to him was unexpectedly rapid and complete. The Hyth, with its storehouses, affording shelter to the besieged, and with its boats* armed with cannon, and moored for the defence of its harbour, ought to have made an efficient and protracted resistance. Its fall, on the very first attack, was the one event of the siege on which the Royalists had cause to reproach themselves. Its defenders showed themselves to be altogether lacking in that spirit and courage which animated their companions. Captain Horsmander, the officer in command, surrendered his post, without an effort, on the first appearance of the enemy. The Hyth (or St. Leonard's) Church, about 300 yards nearer to the town, the next object of Whalley's attack, was at this time a veritable fortress. Marksmen and musqueteers lined its roofs and tower, while a company of loyalist troopers made a stable of its interior for their horses. Its possession was a necessity for a safe military occupancy of the Hyth. Colonel Whalley, confident in his unexpected success, sent forward without delay 300 foot of the Suffolk forces, who, in a fierce hand-to-

* The boats were said to have been so low in the water, by the ebb of the tide, that they could not be made use of in the defence.

hand contest of more than an hour's duration, took
the church by storm.   The Royalist musqueteers
yielded to mercy, while their horse, consisting of
sixty or eighty troopers, chiefly Kentish men, made
good their escape, and entered the town in safety on
the south side, by St. Botolph's Gate.   The previous
barring up of the East Gate by the besiegers had deprived the Hyth of much of its strategic value.   Its
vast storehouses also had long since been denuded of
their treasures, so that the Parliamentarians found in
the Hyth itself " but an empty comb, from which the
honey had been exhausted."   Its capture, however,
hemmed the Royalists within narrower limits, and
enabled Colonel Whalley and his contingent forces
to take possession of the suburbs on the south-east
of the town, and to commence a new line of circumvallation nearer and closer to the walls.

   The second of these attacks, under the direction of
the Commander-in-Chief, proved to be a far more
serious and formidable undertaking.   It involved a
series of manœuvres, strategical tactics, and desperate
struggles, which extended through five long days,
and formed the most remarkable cluster of exciting
events occurring throughout the siege.   In preparation for this grand attack, the Parliamentarian
engineers directed, in the first place, a vigorous
cannonade from Fort Essex against the Royal Fort

erected. by St. Mary's Church. " More powder."
(writes an eye-witness of the scene) "was expended
to-day than in the ten preceding days." The
Royalist leaders discerning the purposes of their foes,
exerted themselves to the utmost to prevent, delay,
and embarrass their proceedings. With much labour
and difficulty they contrived to raise a " saker " to
the belfry platform of St. Mary's Church, that they
might secure a greater elevation, and a longer range
for the service of their cannon. A well-authenticated
tradition prevails that this gun was admirably laid
by an artilleryman, named Thompson,* who had
only one eye, and who caused from this saker much
carnage among the soldiers. This bold manœuvre
on the part of the Royalists succeeded in delaying
the threatened attack. Fairfax withdrew his troops,
and devoted the afternoon of Monday, the 10th, and
the whole of Tuesday, the 11th, of July, by the
advice of his engineers, to the erection of a battery,†

* This Thompson is described in the news-books devoted to the
interests of the Parliament "as an absolute gunner." The belfry of
this church had been previously occupied by a sentinel, who, day and
night, watched and reported the movements of the besiegers.

† A curious incident is recorded as having occurred during the cessation of the Parliamentarian firing for the preparation of their new
battery. "Fourteen exchanged prisoners, marching towards Head Gate,
were fired upon by their own friends from the walls. The mistake was
soon remedied. The prisoners and their escort held up white handker-
chiefs, and were quickly answered from the town by the show of white
flags."

which should obtain a more complete command of
the steeple of St. Mary's Church, and silence the
engine of mischief so lately placed within its
belfry.

On the morning of Wednesday, July 12th, his
artillerymen opened with this new battery on the
devoted belfry of St. Mary's, and on the Royal Fort,
placed below on the platform of the churchyard,
when, to the great joy of the Royalists, and to the
equally great vexation of their foemen, it was quickly
found that the battery was unable to reach with its
iron missives either the balkon or the church.   Fairfax and his colleagues, though chafing at this unexpected delay, renewed their efforts, and devoted two
more days and nights, Wednesday and Thursday, the
12th and 13th of July, to the construction of new
entrenchments and earthworks at a position considerably nearer to the walls.   As the sun declined
on Thursday evening, the engineers of his army
formally announced to Fairfax that their work was
completed, and that they would ensure at last a
successful mastery over the fire of the belfry and of
Fort Royal.   The word of command was passed
throughout the camp that on the morrow the long-
expected attack, so urgently pressed upon Sir Thomas
Fairfax by the members of the Committee of Parliament, would be made in earnest, and that a simul-

taneous effort was to be attempted not only to silence
the Royal Fort, but also to wrest from the Royalists
the two posts of advantage yet held by them without
the walls, viz., the mansion of Sir John Lucas and
the formidable gateway of St. John's Abbey. As
soon as the bright blush of morning ushered in the
dawn of that summer day, Friday, July 14th, the
whole Parliamentarian camp was pervaded with a
confused spirit of inquiry, excitement, and anxiety.
The whole leaguer was to be concerned in the
arrangements. The soldiers of the Tower Hamlet
train-bands and the county of Suffolk forces, encamped on the north and east sides of the town, were
ordered to be on the alert, to watch the gates, and to
assume as threatening an appearance as possible.
The real attack was designed to be made against
the defences on the southern side, and about six
o'clock in the morning the new battery opened fire
on the steeple of St. Mary and its contiguous fort.
The Parliamentarian engineers had this time too
truly calculated their distance, and the guns of the
new entrenchment were soon found to be effective.
After a conflict of some hours, sustained with much
courage on both sides, and when several successive
charges of the two culverins, with which the new
battery was armed, had been fired, the steeple of St.
Mary's, with its belfry platform, fell in ruins to the

ground.   The bells were thrown down, and rents were made in the walls.

At the same hour in the morning another equally severe cannonade had been opened against a portion of the southern defences of the besieged.   A battery, armed with two culverins, constructed against the house of Sir John Lucas, commenced at six o'clock to belch forth its iron shower against the walls.   Hour after hour passed away without any definite issue of the combat.   Every wall, courtyard, and quadrangle was disputed with the utmost desperation.   As fast as breaches were made by the cannon, the Royalists repaired the damage by gabions and sacks of wool, while the soldiers of the Parliament rushed on with equal determination, and in many cases seized the burning wool-sacks with their hands, and carried them away on their shoulders.   Vigorous sallies, too, were made from time to time by the gallant defenders of the mansion, and were as frequently resisted and repulsed.   Every portion of this noble house was at one time or other the scene of continuous hand-to-hand encounters throughout the progress of this eventful day.   It were invidious to single out any one portion of the combatants for special praise, where all behaved as heroes ; yet it is fair to state that the meed of the greatest praise is given by the Parliamentary chroni-

clers to the men of Colonel Barkstead's regiment,
who particularly distinguished themselves in these
personal single combats with their antagonists. So
severe was the conflict that the horse regiments
under Fairfax's personal command were ordered up
in support of their friends ; and this incident is nar-
rated by a participant in the fight : " A trooper was
slain, but, notwithstanding, the horse was true to his
trust, and ran home without his rider."

Late in the afternoon of this hard-fought day, the
breaches made by the cannon in the walls were pronounced by the engineers to be practicable for an
assault ; and Fairfax ordered that an effort should be
made to win possession of the mansion by storm.
At about six o'clock in the evening, the Parliamentarian soldiers, drawn chiefly from Colonel Barkstead's and Colonel Ewers' brave regiments, approached
the breaches in force. After a desperate contest,
shoulder to shoulder, and pike to pike, the power of
greater numbers prevailed. It was a fight such as
only Englishmen could have waged. The Royalists,
however, at last, driven from courtyard to courtyard,
and from chamber to chamber, evacuated the mansion,
and secured for themselves, as the sun set, a shelter
and refuge in the fortified Gate-house of St. John's
Abbey. The Parliamentarian soldiers played extraordinary havoc with the prize thus won at so much

expenditure of labour and such ample effusion of blood. They not only ransacked the house of its treasures, and enriched themselves with its spoils, but they gathered its palatial furniture, its oaken tables, gorgeous tapestries, curiously cut chairs, its stuffs, books, and pictures, its strange heterogeneous mixture of beds and mats and kitchen goods, and with them made a conflagration, which terminated in the destruction by fire of a considerable portion of the mansion.

Such were the issues of the most disastrous day which had yet befallen the Royalists since they possessed themselves of the town of Colchester. Notwithstanding all their courage and determination, they had to lament a double loss in the destruction of their most effective battery on the balkon and at St. Mary's, and in their compulsory abandonment of their strongest outpost, the house of Sir John Lucas. Other yet severer trials were at hand. Fairfax, vastly inspirited by a success equalling his highest expectations, and stirred up by the presence of the Parliament's Commissioners, avowed himself not contented to " occupy Sir John Lucas's house, and to allow the defeated Royalists to play the porter at his gate." He determined to crown his late successes with new victories, to drive, without the loss of a day, the enemy from his present stronghold, and to gain possession of the Gate-house of St. John's

F

Abbey. This was confessedly a formidable under·
taking. The Gate-house of St. John was not commanded by the artillery of any of his batteries or
entrenchments. It was a small citadel in itself, and
afforded its defenders the advantage of shooting from
an elevated position, and under the shelter of walls
and parapets ; and, if captured at all, could only be
captured by storm, and by the personal valour of his
soldiers. Fairfax determined to act without delay,
and ordered an immediate assault on the post held by
the retreating Royalists. The morning of Saturday,
July 15th, was spent in the preparation of scaling-
ladders, and of all things required for a storming
party. The scaling-ladders provided were of ample
dimensions, being twenty rounds, or about 24 feet
in height and 6 feet in width, so that six men could
mount them abreast.*

The attack commenced about three o'clock in the
afternoon by the approach of the " forlorn hope," a
brave band of volunteers, carrying their ladders, and
attended by a party of musqueteers of Colonel Ewers'
regiment. A terrible conflict ensued. " We have

---

* Bourne, " Inventions or Devises," p. 48, gives an account of the
construction of these ladders. He says : " And six men may stand and
fight upon the top of every one of these ladders, and handle his
weapon "—so that evidence is hereby afforded to prove that General
Fairfax acted in these arrangements strictly in accordance with the
authoritatively taught engineering principles of his times.

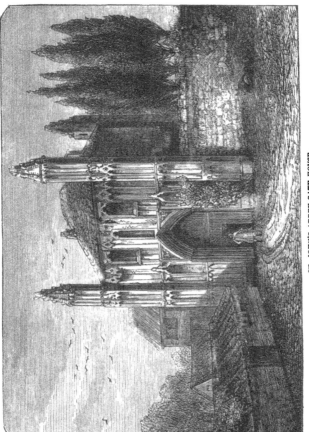

ST. JOHN'S ABBEY GATE-HOUSE.

Siege of Colchester, page 66.

stormed " (writes a Parliamentarian chronicler) " one
of their strongest fortifications, but before we could
gain it we had a hard disputation.   They knocked us
off our ladders, and threw down great stones and
brickbats upon us, and defended it with great resolution, till at the last our men set to their ladders again,
and up they went with great fury, and got up to the
battlements of the Gate-house, casting grenados *
out of their hands over amongst the soldiers."   The
agony of this struggle was not to be compared with
that on the preceding day.   Though sharp for the
time, it was exceedingly brief ; for about five o'clock,
two hours after the commencement of the engagement, a grenade, or lighted fire-ball thrown by the
hand, fell into the powder magazine of the Royalists.
A fearful explosion followed, and the defenders of the
gateway being thus deprived of the means of continu-
ing their resistance, retired into the town.   In their

* "Grenados, or hollow breaking balls of various sorts — fireballs
for divers uses, as to sticke, and burn combustible objects, burne, breake,
poison, or blind the enemy, burn in the water, or pierce the flesh to the
bone.   Some are made of baked potters' clay, of glass, or canvas, coated
and armed.   The receits are also divers—as powder, 4 ozs.; sulphur,
2 ozs.; saltpetre, 12 oz.; finely beaten and well mixed.   These may
be loaded with bullets, stones, nails, shot, and such like.   These are of
great execution, but must ever be so provided, that the slow fire must
be sure to burne untill the ball fired be arrived at the place where
it is to doe its execution.   Of this kind there are infinite diversities
and inventions."—See " The Gunner's Dialogue," by Robert Norton
pp. 87, 88.   London, 1643.

retreat to the gates, partly in self-defence, partly in
exasperation at their successive losses, and partly in
revenge for the firing of Sir John Lucas's house, they
set fire to the houses in the suburbs extending from
St. Botolph's Priory to North Gate, on the south and
south-west frontage of the town. " And presently "
(writes a witness of the scene) " began that fearful
sight and woeful spectacle of firing all round the
walls, the streets on both sides (of the Head Gate)
being set on fire ; and from the time of the taking of
the Gate-house, all that night for about a mile in
length continued burning and flaming, that some of
us, being a mile distant, had light almost to read a
letter so far, and a terrible, red, dusky cloud seemed
to hang over the town all night ; and so furious was
the fire by reason such stately and goodly buildings
were burnt thereby, that many times the flashes
mounted aloft, far above houses, churches, or any
buildings, and continued with such horrors, crack-
lings heard a mile or two from the town, and with
such lamentable outcries of men, women, and children, that it is beyond description."

CHAPTER VI.

A CHAPTER ON MILITARY AFFAIRS.

> . . . . " Chain'd thunderbolts and hail
> Of iron globes."
>   MILTON.

First standing army in England—The train-bands of the City of London
—The cost of the Parliamentarian army—Charges for provisions—
Amount of expenditure during the siege—An account of the pike
and musquet—The artillery of Sir Thomas Fairfax—Ufano—English
engineers—Conduct of sieges of towns—Triumph of engineers—
Mode of conveying cannon—Military punishments—Dangers of civil
warfare—Specimen of passes of Fairfax.

THE army, marshalled by the Parliament during the
civil war, and commanded first by the Earl of Essex,
and then by Sir Thomas Fairfax, was the first example
of a standing or permanent army in England.
Previously to the outbreak of the civil war the protection of the island against foreign invasion was
secured by the ships of the Royal fleet, which were
commissioned for the summer months in each year,
and provided as in later times the first line of the
national defences; and then by a Militia summoned
to assemble in cases of emergency by the Royal com-

mand, or by virtue (as it was called) of the King's
Commission of Array.

This militia consisted of "train-bands," chiefly
raised in London, and in the large towns, seaport or
inland, and of regiments of yeomanry contributed by
the counties. The train-bands of London had their
own organisation and special regulations for the conduct of their services. They formed six several regiments, composed for the most part of the apprentices
and artisans of the cities of Westminster and London.
Created and supported at the charges of the wealthier
citizens, distinguished by the different colours of their
uniforms—red, white, green, blue, buff, or orange—
strengthened in every crisis by the unanimity of
political sympathies, or by the ties of local associa-
tion, they formed a prominent feature and took an
active part in the struggles of this eventful period.
They were remarkable throughout the war for their
enmity to the King, and for their fidelity to the Parliament, to whom at several times they rendered
valuable assistance. The City train-bands raised the
siege of Gloucester, won the doubtful honours of the
second battle of Newbury, and claimed the privilege
of providing a guard for the House of Commons, of
manning the walls, and defending the lines, redoubts,
and entrenchments with which London was surrounded
during the early period of this contest. One of these

train-bands, known by the name of "The Tower" or "Green" regiment, was present at the siege of Colchester, and bore its full portion of the burden and protracted labours of that conflict.

The standing army of the Parliament involved a considerable outlay. War, in those days, as in the present, could only be waged at a great cost. The pay and rations of the officers and soldiers, with the price of forage for the horses of the troopers, were regulated by various ordinances of Parliament. The cavalry soldier was entitled to have what hay his horse could eat for 4d. a night, and grass at 2d. a night. He was to be supplied with oats at 4d., and with beans or peas at 6d. a peck. The innkeeper was required to provide "dyett," food and lodging, for "every trooper or horseman" at 8d.; for every dragooner at 7d.; and for every foot-soldier, pioneer, or waggoner at 6d. the day. Every officer holding a commission, or "any person of Lifeguard," was ordered to pay the full value of his provisions for horse and man. If by want of pay he could not at the time satisfy the full demand of the innkeeper, he was required, under strict penalties, to give a ticket distinctly stating the amount of the food or accommodation he had received, and the charges made for the same. The money value of these tickets was paid at some later time by the commissaries of the

Parliament. The expenses of the army so long detained at Colchester were estimated at £4,000 a
week. At the conclusion of the siege the inhabitants
of the county of Essex presented to Parliament in the
spring of 1649 a petition, in which they asked for an
exemption from the taxation imposed on the various
counties of England, on the plea that they had incurred large expenses in the victualling and maintenance of the army before Colchester. This petition
was rejected; as it was proved before a Committee
of the House of Commons, by the production of
the corresponding receipts, that after the termination of the siege a sum exceeding £300,000 was paid
by the Commissioners of the Parliament to persons
resident in the county on account of the supplies provided to the army during its location at Colchester.*

The infantry regiments formed the greater portion
of the army at this time, and as they bore the brunt
of the conflict, so they chiefly reaped the honours of
the victory. These regiments were formed of two
separate classes of soldiers, the pikemen and the
musqueteers. The pike was a formidable weapon.

* The Parliament sanctioned this scale of pay to the officers and
soldiers of their horse regiments in February, 1647 :—A colonel of horse,
12s. a day ; a major, 5s. ; a preacher, 6s. ; a provost-marshal, 3s. 4d. ;
his two men, 2s. 6d. ; a chyrurgeon, 4s., and a mate (attendant) 2s. 6d. ;
a colonel as captain, 10s. ; a lieutenant, 5s., his two horses, 2s. 4d. ; a
quarter-master, 4s. ; a corporal and trumpeter, 2s. 6d. ; smith and
saddle cart, 2s. 4d.

It was made of a long staff or pole, terminating in a strong iron-pointed head, eight or ten inches in length, and furnished at the side with a very sharp knife-like blade. Armed with this weapon the soldiers entered into close combat, and fought hand-to-hand, "at push of pike"* as it was called. The fight frequently lasted through the greater part of a day, without any great loss of life on either side ; as the combatants would stand with their weapons locked against each other, and strain with all their might to push their foemen by their bodily strength from off the field. The final victory was gained by those

* The following "Devise" for a successful encounter with this weapon may possibly amuse. At all events it will illustrate the mode of warfare generally in use during the civil war :—

"Suppose that the front of both battels is pikes, and the one as many men in a rancke as the other, yet it is possible that the one may overthrow the other at the first meeting of the battell without any recoverie, by means of the order of the fighting, as this : The one battell cometh according unto the accustomable manner, thinking to stand at the pushe of the pike with them, and the other battell coming in that forme in like manner, untill that they are in a manner hard unto them, and then upon the suddaine they doo all the fore front run in narrower and together so close as they can, coming in shoulder unto shoulder, and then the ranckes that are behinde, for the quantitie of neare the half of the battell doeth the like, and so dooth come close unto the backe of them that are before, and so running with great violence, and the poyntes of their pikes forwards, that they must pearce and enter the front of the other battell, for they that are before must needes run into them, for they that are behinde doo force them in, and they that are of the other battell must needes give way or else fall downe and be troden under feete, and then, if that they bee once separated and put out of their order, they must needes be overthrowne without any recovery."— Bourne's " Rare Inventions and Strange Devises," p. 79. London, 1578.

with whom rested the greatest physical strength, and
the more patient discipline of endurance.

The musqueteer regiments were armed with a very
different weapon from the modern rifle, pouring in
its deadly fusillade at the distance of a mile. The
musquet of these times carried its bullet to only a
short distance, and had neither flint, copper-cap, nor
needle point. It was fired by a match, a long combustible cord or string prepared to smoulder and
keep alight, and applied directly by the hand to the
touch-hole. The failure of the match was the great
risk which the soldier had to guard against.

The artillery provided to the army of Sir Thomas
Fairfax was equally defective when compared with the
wonderful perfection of modern engineers. It is not
improbable that our great poet Milton, in his description of the combat of the Satanic hosts, gave an ac-
curate picture of the artillery in common use at the
time in which he lived :

> " A triple mounted row of pillars laid
> On wheels (for like to pillars most they seem'd),
> Or hollow bodies made of oak or fir,
> With branches lopt, in wood or mountain fell'd,
> Brass, iron, stony mould, had not their mouths
> With hideous orifice gaped on us wide,
> Portending hollow truce ; at each behind
> A seraph stood, and in his hand a reed
> Stood waving, tipt with fire, while we, suspense,
> Collected stood within our thoughts amused
> Not long ; for sudden all at once their reeds
> Put forth, and to a narrow vent applied

With nicest touch. Immediately in a flame
But soon obscured with smoke, all heaven appear'd,
From those deep-throated engines belch'd, whose roar
Embowell'd with outrageous noise the air,
And all her entrails tore, disgorging foul
Their devilish glut, chained thunderbolts and hail
Of iron globes, which on the victor host
Levell'd, with such impetuous fury smote,
That whom they hit, none on their feet might stand,
Though standing else as rocks."

The "master-gunners," as the chief engineer
officers were called in the middle of the seventeenth
century, were barely acquainted with the rudiments
of scientific warfare, and little versed in the practical
handling of artillery. The one great master of the
art, by whose work* all the military engineers throughout Europe were at this period instructed, was Ufano,
an Italian, Governor of the citadel of Antwerp, who
had served in the army of the Duke of Alva in Flanders at the close of the preceding century. Two
English engineers, William Bourne,† a scientific
master-gunner, in command for some time of Deal
Castle, and John Eldred, for fifty years chief gunner at
Dover Castle, had transferred to their own treatises
the rules and directions of Ufano, and their works were

* " Artillerie : vraie Instruction de l'artillerie de toutes ses apparten-
ances." Par Diego Ufano, Capitaine de l'artillerie; traduit en langue
francoise, par Jean Theodore de Bry. Frankfort, 1614.

† " Inventions or Devises: very necessary for all Generalles and
Captaines, or Leaders of men, as well by sea as by land." Written by
William Bourne. An. 1578. London : printed for Thomas Woodcock,
dwelling in Paule's Churchyard, at the signe of the Black Beare.

at this period the great authorities by whom English
artillerists were taught and instructed in the mysteries
of their profession. The two great impediments to
be overcome by the master-gunners of this day were
the uncertainty of the aim, and the difficulty of rightly
"disparting,"* or calculating the allowance necessary
to be made in firing, partly for the elevation, and
partly for the varying degrees of thickness in the different portions of the gun.

The accompanying schedule,† taken from Eldred's

Name of Piece.	Weight of Piece.	Diameter of Shot.	Weight of Shot.	Weight of Powder.	Length of Piece.	Point blank Distance.	Distance of Shot thrown at 10 degrees of elevation.
	lbs.	ins.	lbs.	lbs.	feet.	yards	yards.
Saker	2,500	2½	5¼	6	9½	360	2,170
Demi-Culverin......	2,700	4	10	10	10	400	2,400
Culverin	4,500	5½	18	18	12—15	440	2,650
Demi-Canon	6,000	6¼	35	26	10	380	1,902
Canon ordinary	7,500	7¾	64	42	11½	340	2,000
Double or Royal Cannon............	8,000	8	70	46	12	400	2,400

"Gunner's Glass," gives the names of the pieces
in most common use during the civil war. It also
supplies in a simple and succinct form the weight
of the gun, the quantity of powder required for its

* The "Dispart" is half the difference between the diameter of
the gun at the base ring and at the swell of the muzzle. Griffith's
"Artillerist's Manual," p. 50. London, 1852.
† "The Gunner's Glass." By William Eldred. London, 1646. See
pp. 88, 94, 96.

discharge, the weight of the shot, and the distance to which the gun will carry at point blank, and at ten degrees of elevation.

It appears from this schedule* that the artillery in ordinary use at this time could carry a shot from a mile to a mile and a-quarter. The master-gunners, however, endeavoured to place their heavy ordnance for the battering of walls about a third of a mile from the object of attack. Engineering warfare, as a real science, is of comparatively modern growth. The present "Krupp" or "Armstrong" guns surpass those used in the sieges of the Commonwealth in every particular—in powder, ball, sighting, and elevation; in the superiority of rapid firing, of certain aim, of increased power in devastation, of facility in locomotion, of strength in material, and of beauty in construction.

The English engineers, Eldred, Bourne, and Thomas Smith† are very minute in their instructions for the

* In Molesworth's "Pocket Book," cast iron (of which these balls were made) is stated to weigh ·225 to ·273 lbs. per cubic foot; and according to that statement, the relative reckoning in this schedule of the diameter and weight of the shot will be found approximately correct. The correctness of the schedule in one particular is a presumptive argument confirming the accuracy of the whole.

† Another treatise, written by an English artillerist of repute, must be added to those of Bourne and Eldred. Thomas Smith, a soldier in the garrison of Berwick, under the command of Lord Willoughby, Lord Warden of the Marches, wrote the "Art of Gunnery." London, 1648. This volume is the most practical of these treatises. Smith

conduct of sieges of towns. The highest triumph
of their art seems to have been the concentration of
the fire of six cannon at once on some chosen spot in
the wall of a blockaded town. The following extract
will explain the manner of proceeding :—

" Give level with one piece below at the bottom of
the wall, and with the next piece a foot higher right
over that, and with the third right a foot over that,
saving that you need to give the level unto no piece
more than three-quarters the height of the wall, and
then in like manner give the level with your pieces at
the other part of your battery unto that place that
the other part was laid against, within a fathom or
more at your discretion, so that the one place may
flank, or beat against the other, crossing in the middle of the wall. And when you doe mean to shoot
them off, then give fire unto them all at once, at both
the places, that they may all beat, and shake the
wall at one time together, and then it will beat it
down, or shake it down all the faster, and the bottom
being broken away, the top will fall away of itself, and
so when you have broken the wall, and still do make
it wider, then give level at your discretion upon the

directs (p. 44) "That the ordnance should be planted within 200 or
240 paces of the object to be overthrowne, if it be possible to have
convenient platformes and to bring them so nigh the said object."
N.B.—A thousand paces were reckoned to the mile, p. 31.

wall, observing the order before rehersed, both in the levelling, and of the giving fire unto the pieces." *

The next chapter will afford evidence that the engineers of the besiegers at Colchester scrupulously adhered to these instructions of firing at the walls a simultaneous discharge of six cannon.

The movement of these great guns from their various places of deposit to the besieged towns was in these days a work of immense labour. There were but few high-roads, and the route from one town to another frequently lay across commons and open fields. These guns were drawn for the most part by oxen, and often from fourteen to seventeen couple † of these animals were attached to a single gun. The great guns brought to the siege of Colchester were thus conveyed. A whole fortnight elapsed before they could be brought from the Tower of London to the camp of Sir Thomas Fairfax.

The army under the command of Sir Thomas Fairfax, although partaking of a civilian character, was subject to severe discipline. The two modes of punishment in most common use were riding the " wooden horse," and "running the gauntlet." The first of these

* " Art of Shooting in Great Ordnance." Written by William Bourne. Imprinted at London for Thomas Woodcock, 1587. Chapter xix. p. 64.

" 17 yoak of oxen are sufficient for the draught of a canon of 8000 lbs. weight."—" The Art of Gunnery," by Thomas Smith, p. 51.

was the placing the offender for an hour on a wooden
form, constructed in the shape of the stands on
which saddles are usually placed in a modern stable,
and suspending a musquet to each heel instead
of a spur. The painful punishment was found to
cause so much bodily injury that it was soon dismissed from the list of military punishments. The
following account of running the gauntlet, taken from
a news-book of the day, December 6, 1648, will
best describe this punishment. " Two soldiers, Mat-
hew and Robert Roe, were condemned ' to run the
gauntlope ' through Colonel Deane's regiment. The
whole regiment are to stand one by one, halfe on one
side, and halfe on the other, and every one with a
wand or switch in his hand, and these two to be
stripped naked to the waist, and so to pass along
through all the soldiers of the regiment, and every
one to have a stroke at each of them." Nor was their
punishment at all too severe for the offence. They
had forged a certificate demanding of a citizen £200
as a levy on his goods towards the charges of the war.
The citizens complained to the officer in command,
and succeeded in obtaining redress. The place appointed for the scene of this punishment was the front
of the Royal Exchange, in the City of London.

Not only, however, were the citizens of London,
and the inhabitants of the large provincial towns, sub-

ject to these acts of unlicensed marauding, but the country through its whole length and breadth was in a state of extremest misery and confusion during the whole period of the war. A regular sum of many thousand pounds was exacted as a monthly contribution from the various counties of England for the maintenance of the army. The country squires and the gentry were especially the sufferers. Whichever side they took they were in danger. If they avowed themselves to be the friends either of the King or the Parliament, they were exposed to the attacks of the army hostile to the interests they favoured. If they observed an impartial neutrality, and abstained from any active interference on either side, they were still liable to domiciliary visits from military commissaries, and of requisitions for food, or arms, or money. These evils, which prevailed in greater force in the protracted stages of the first war, from 1642 to 1646, between the King and the Parliament, were in this second civil war considerably modified. Many of the loyal squires and magistrates had compounded by the payment of fines and penalties, and were now left in quiet possession of the remnant of their estates. The chief danger at this time was to be feared by travellers, especially by those who were suspected of treachery or hostility to the Parliament. To secure these persons from harm, more particularly

G

when returning from places in revolt against the Parliament, Sir Thomas Fairfax instituted a system of passes, the possessor of which was ensured of safety and protection from all under his authority. A frequent mention of these passes occurs in the narrative of the siege; and the form in which they were issued will supply a fitting conclusion to this chapter.

Form of Pass.

" Sir Thomas Fairfax, Knight, Generall of the forces " of the Parliament.

" Suffer the bearer, A. B., who was in the city [or garrison] of C., to pass your guards quietly without let or interruption, with his servants, horses, arms, goods, and all other necessaries, and to repaire to ———, upon his necessary occasions, and in all places where he may reside, or whereunto he shall remove, be protected from all violence to his person, goods, and estate, and to have full liberty at any time within the space of six months to repaire to any convenient fort, and to transport himself, with his servants, goods, and necessaries, beyond seas. Hereunto due obedience is to be given by all persons whom it may concern, as they will answer to the contrary. Given under my hand and seale.

　　　　　　　　　　" FAIRFAX.

" To all officers and souldiers under my command ; and to all others whom it may concerne."

CHAPTER VII.

DIURNAL OF SIEGE, FROM THE CAPTURE OF ST. JOHN'S
GATEWAY AND THE BURNING OF THE SUBURBS, TO
THE TERMINATION OF THE SIEGE—FROM JULY 16TH
TO AUGUST 27TH.

" And registered by Fame Eternal
In deathless pages of Diurnal."
Hudibras, Part I., Canto iii., 20.

Diurnal of siege—Refusal to admit Sir Thomas Fairfax's trumpeter—
Sir Charles Lucas's horse shot under him—A courageous boy—Attempt
to escape—Treachery of townsmen—A flight of arrows—"Sair"
hearts at Colchester—A horse roasted—Preparations against a storming—Corps of dismounted troopers—A premium on cannon balls—
Repulse at Middle Mill—A brave ensign—A successful stratagem—
A Fabian policy—A second slaughter of horses—A sad accident—
Reduction of allowance of bread—A letter about exchange of
prisoners—Good service of scythemen—Encouraging letter from
Sir Marmaduke Langdale—Intense sufferings—Dogs, cats, mice, and
rats killed and eaten—An acceptable collation—An affecting interview—A windmill on the castle—Firing of houses—Starch and
currant puddings—A bloody sally—A despairing mother—General
Fairfax in danger—A fight for a dead horse—Inhabitants required to
leave the town—Last search for food in the town—Permission to pass
asked by the inhabitants of Fairfax—Unsuccessful mediation of
Parliament's Committee—Ultimatum of Royalists—Mine at East Gate
—Proposal to fight a way out abandoned—Final negotiations—Letter
of surrender—Conclusion.

THE events recorded in the fifth chapter, the fierce
and protracted disputes for the possession of Sir John
Lucas's house, the fiery attack and as spirited resist-

ance attendant on the conquest of St. John's Gate-
house, the burning the houses in the suburbs, with
the capture of the Hyth, the silencing the Royal Fort,
and the destruction of St. Mary's Church, exhausted
the strength and abated the fury alike of the besiegers
and besieged.

Whatever were the cause, the siege from this time
forward dragged on an equal and a comparatively un-
exciting course. The foemen on either side learnt to
respect the courage and determination of each other.
If, however, there be any truth in the opinion that
passive and patient endurance is a more real test of the
perfection of human courage than any active exertion,
then will the remaining part of this history abound in
interest, as it will afford ample testimony to an almost
superhuman heroism under severe, prolonged, and ac-
cumulated sufferings. The remaining weeks of the
siege will best be told in a form of a journal, in which
is recorded, day by day, some event and incident
which actually occurred. The author cannot lay
claim to having found this journal in the very shape
in which it is now printed. It is, however, constructed from materials related in the " news-books,
fly-leaves," and other publications of the day, and is
supposed to have been kept by a Royalist citizen of
Colchester as a diary of the events and circumstances
as they happened in the town or camp. The lan-

guage may seem quaint and old-fashioned. The
author thought it would be more real if he were to
use the very words themselves of the contemporary
chroniclers, and not to translate them into more
modern forms of expression. Not a single incident is
invented or exaggerated. The diary is a faithful account, such as a witness might have written, day by
day, of the scenes and circumstances passing before
his eyes, as they actually occurred.

" DIURNAL OF THE SIEGE KEPT BY A ROYALIST
CITIZEN OF COLCHESTER.

" Sunday, July 16.—Sir Thomas Fairfax, in the
hope that we were disheartened by our losses, sends a
trumpeter to demand the surrender of the town, and
to endeavour to tamper with our soldiers, by offering
them terms independent of their commanders. This
conduct, so opposed to the usual conditions of honourable warfare, greatly exasperated our officers.
The trumpeter is consequently denied admission at
all the gates. At the East Gate Sir Charles Lucas
demands, from the parapet, the purport of his message; and on his telling it, dismisses him with the
threat of a 'gibbet' if he should again be the bearer
of such offers to his soldiers.

" Monday, July 17.—The Tower regiment is moved
by Fairfax from the east bridge to the centre of his

northern line of investment. Colonel Rainsborough, the third* commander since the commencement of the siege, rode at its head. Mrs. Buxton and one other gentlewoman allowed to leave the town this day, with a pass from General Sir Thomas Fairfax.

"Tuesday, July 18.—Before the *réveille* had been beat, Sir Charles Lucas sallied out in person with General Hastings, Colonel Lunsford, and divers other persons of quality, with about 400 horse and 800 foot. A severe volley from the enemy caused them to retreat; but they immediately rallied, and went on again, insomuch that there happened a sharp dispute betwixt both parties, and continued for the space of a quarter of an hour. Sir Charles's horse was shot under him, and divers on both sides wounded.

"About four o'clock in the afternoon our great guns fire for an hour against Fort Essex. We kill a matrose† at the Great Mount, and wound some few, and dismount one of their pieces, splitting the muzzle. The enemy answered with spirit and gave three shots for our one. They played *six pieces*‡ all together for the space of two hours against the Royal Fort.

* Colonels Needham and Shambrooke had been killed before the town, pp. 25, 51.

† A matrose was the name of the assistants to the gunner.

‡ This firing of six cannon all together was according to the strict rules of artillery practice in those days. See proceding chapter, p. 78. The

" Wednesday, July 19.—An incident occurred to-day, which showed that the determined resolution of our soldiers was shared in by the children. A boy of little stature, much wit, and desperate resolution was sent out privately this evening with letters from the Governor (Lord Norwich). The enemy's sentinel perceived him, and brought him up to the Lord General's quarters. Upon search no letters to be found; upon examination confessed nothing. They tempted him with gold, but that not prevailing, threatened him with hanging, and, that as fruitless, burnt his fingers with match, and, still resolved, pulled him up; all in vain. At length he told them, ' The Lord Governor and his father bid him be hanged or suffer any other death than confess his business, or discover anything concerning his letters, which he was resolved to do.' He remains a prisoner with the Marshal-General.

" Thursday, July 20.—The enemy this day finished their line of batteries from St. Botolph's to North Gate, and planted their ordnance; but cannot bombard the town till their waggons, which have been despatched to London for more ammunition, return to camp. Our commanders bring all their horse, and a great part of their foot, at night into the castle-yard, and march out of the town by the bridge they had

old fort was the fort on the balkon, which had been again rendered serviceable since the attack on the morning of Friday the 14th instant.

constructed between Middle Hill and North Gate—
hoping to have effected an escape. The night was
dark, and they past the bridge without discovery;
but their guides and pioneers, who were for the most
part townsmen, agreeable to a plotted combination
between them, ran away, and so they were compelled
to retreat into the town. The suburbs near the
North Gate were set on fire by the Parliamentarians
in their vexation at our safe return. As the conflagration commenced, they fired six pieces at our
walls, and continued to play them for some time.

" Friday, June 21.—A quantity of arrows were shot
into the town with labels, and letters promising money
and pardon, and passes to all soldiers who would
desert their colours and submit to the Lord General.

" Saturday, July 22.—There is many a sad and
sair heart in Colchester to-day. The first care of a
good trooper is his charger, and the result is that a
mysterious sympathy and affection often spring up
between the horse and his rider. The Council of
War orders that all the horses be assembled in the
bailey,* or ditch of the castle. The summons being
obeyed, the third part of every troop was drawn out
and assigned to the commissary, that he might kill
some for immediate eating, and ' powder ' the rest for
future victuals.

* Bailey, from Latin word *ballivum*, a ditch or trench.

"Sunday, July 23.—How great is the difference between contemplation and action under calamity! the men who wept yesterday at the proposal to kill their horses, are to-day making merry at the eating them! The troopers, amidst much rough merriment, roast a horse whole near the main guard in Head Gate. The Governor and some of the commanders attend, and eat some slices, and distribute wine to drink the King's health.

"Monday, July 24.—The storming of the town is daily expected. The enemy will meet with a warm reception. Large deep holes are dug in all the streets to impede the enemy's horse, the High Street alone excepted, as in it the troopers feed the horses that remain, upon the stalls belonging to the shops. The troopers who have been dismounted are formed into companies of footmen, and are armed with scythes placed edgeways on long poles.*   Lord Arthur Capel is their commander, and walks at their head with his halberd shouldered. As the ammunition is

* The Parliamentary news-books of the day call the Royalist troops "Shavers," from their being armed with these scythes. It was a formidable weapon of offence. It was subsequently used by some of the followers of Prince Charles Edward.   At the battle of Preston "a small party of McGregors, bearing for their only arms the blades of scythes fastened end-long upon poles, clove heads to the chin, cut off the legs of horses, and even, it is said, laid the bodies of men in two distinct pieces upon the field."—Chambers's "History of Rebellion in Scotland." Note i., p. 158.

scarce he offers 6*d.* for every bullet, and a shilling for
every cannon ball that is picked up and brought him.
Trenches are dug behind the walls to harass and stop
the stormers. Barrels of tar and pitch are provided,
and fires to heat the same, with frying-pans to cast it
hot on the heads of the soldiers if they approach to
storm.

" Tuesday, July 25.—A general alarm was made
along the whole line of the enemy in dead of night, as
if a storm was intended ; but the north side of the
town alone became, for the first time, the scene of
active strife. Colonel Rainsborough, with the Tower
regiment, advanced at midnight from his new fort,
commanding the ford of the river, close to the middle
mill, and attempted to set it on fire. It is the only
mill we have remaining. His attack was no sooner
discovered than defeated, chiefly by a party of gentlemen who were on guard, and who attacked them
with such spirit and resolution, that they not only
failed in their design, but were forced to such a hasty
and disorderly retreat, that many of the men missing
the ford were drowned, on perceiving which our
men fired but little, but beat their kettles in scorn,
and afterwards their drums in defiance of them.

" This gallant repulse was not achieved without loss;
a brave young lad, an ensign in Col. Till's regiment,
was shot through the body—in at one side and out at

the other—with a five-pound bullet, after which he
went from the guard to his quarters in the town by
the help of a soldier who led him, and being laid on
his bed, he died, expressing only the wish that he
had been shot with his colours in his hand, that so
his friends might have the more believed that he
loved the King, and cheerfully died in his defence.

"Wednesday, July 26.—*Expectata dies aderat.*
The Parliamentarians commenced early this morning
a cannonade against the town, and battered the walls
from North Gate to Head Gate. They did not cause
much damage. Our soldiers sally out in force, and
attack their entrenchments. They advanced and
charged with much fury. The action was disputed
by both parties with much courage.

"Thursday, July 27.—Sir Thomas Fairfax com-
mences a new fort in the Berry Fields, between
St. Mary Magdalen Church and the walls, in order
that he may bring his line nearer the town, between
St. Botolph Gate and East Gate. Our men, in their
determination to dispute to the last the enemy's advance, make a smart sally and beat the soldiers and
workmen off the new fort, and follow them to the
street leading to the Hyth. This sortie took place at
noonday. The Parliamentarians approaching in great
bodies of horse and foot, our men retire.

"Friday, July 28.—Colonel Scroope was despatched

to-day with his three troops of light horse to Yarmouth, to assist in garrisoning that town, on the
rumoured arrival of the Prince of Wales with the
fleet to compel it to surrender.

" Saturday, July 29.—Colonel Whalley snapped
up some horses grazing beneath the walls. They
were thirty-eight in number, by no means serviceable,
unless good keeping recover them. The few remaining horses were often the cause of short but stubborn
conflicts. The forage being all gone, the only means
of preserving life in them was by the grass outside
the walls. The troopers obtain this at the hazard of
their lives, going out in parties, some of whom keep
guard against the enemy while others cut the grass.

" Sunday, July 30.—Sir William Masham was exchanged for Mr. John Ashburnham, by the especial
direction of the Parliament. Sir William was received by his servant at Head Gate, and expressed
great joy at his deliverance.

" Monday, July 31.—A stratagem was practised
with partial success. A party last night sallied out
to discover the nature of some new works in the
course of construction. Twenty carried spades, and
the same number muskets. They passed the first
sentinel, saying, ' they were come to finish the work,
where they had wrought the preceding night.' With
the second guard they engaged, and after killing

several, brought away Captain Gray, the officer in command. The enemy is so near to us at East Gate that our men call to their men and interchange many words of mutual violence and reproach."

The siege relapsed at the end of this month into a chronic state of laborious inactivity. Day followed day with little variety. Fairfax pursued his Fabian policy, and declined to storm, in mercy to the townsmen as he alleged, but more probably from the conviction that if his troops ventured on the attack—

> " Repulse
> Repeated, and indecent overthrow
> Doubled, would render them yet more despised,
> And to their foes a laughter."

The Royalists, amidst their privations, held on with a bulldog courage, which, though powerless to conquer, refused to yield.

" Tuesday, August 1.—About two o'clock in the afternoon our men gave a great shout to alarm the enemy, which they soon after answered with another shout, but no action was done by the sword at that time.

" Wednesday, August 2.—A second rendezvous of all the horses is ordered in the castle-yard. The officers are strictly enjoined not to conceal their horses. Certain of the fattest in each troop are given over to the commissary.

" Thursday, August 3.—A search for arms is instituted in the town. A large number of brown
bill-hooks are found, and the dismounted men are
armed with these, and march cheerfully under their
leaders.

" Friday, August 4.—A soldier came into the town,
saying 'that he had come from Sir M. Langdale's
army, who would himself come to help us within
seven days.' Upon examination he was found to be
one of Ireton's troopers who had some distaste from
his commander. On discovering who he was, he was
clapped into a dungeon, and was not allowed to
escape.

" In the evening of this day did Mr. John Good-
wyn, Mr. Price, Mr. Lavender, and Mr. Overton (the
bookseller), ride about our line, and Mr. Overton
passing over a foot-bridge, the planks being slippery,
down he fell horse and man. The river being
swelled,* the man is lost, and his body not yet
found.

" Saturday, August 5.—The allowance of bread is
abated from fourteen ounces to ten ounces a-day.
A trumpeter brings this letter from Sir Thomas
Fairfax in reference to an exchange of prisoners

* An extraordinary storm is spoken of at this time in the news-books.
" The wind at north-east with abundance of rain, which hath not only
driven away very much hay by land-floods, but spoiled much corn upon
the ground, and bloweth up trees by the roots."

which Lord Norwich and the commander had omitted
to complete :—

" ' MY LORDS,

" ' I cannot but wonder I have no returne from
you concerning the exchange of Ensign Carrington
and the corporal, having formerly sent you three
towards them, which you neither returned nor sent
out any in exchange for them, and having by the last
drum sent in three more according to your desire to
compleat that exchange, I desire you to send them
forth by this drum, as also your answer concerning
the exchange according to the list sent you in my
last. Your prisoners shall be ready at three of the
clock this afternoon, at the alms-houses, to be delivered to any drum you shall send for them, if you
send notice that the prisoners you have of mine in
exchange be there ready at the same time to come
forth.

" ' Yr servant,

" ' FAIRFAX.

" ' 5th August, 1648.
" ' FOR THE LORD NORWICH, LORD CAPELL,
        AND CHARLES LUCAS.'

" Sunday, August 6.—A quiet day. There was

scarcely a cannon or musquet heard within or without
the walls.

"Monday, August 7.—Our whole army is in motion.
The Council of War determines on a general charge
on the enemy. Our men make a simultaneous sally
from all the five main gates in the hope of breaking
through the leaguer. Sir Charles Lucas led the van,
and exchanged a brace of bullets with Colonel
E. Whalley. Our scythemen did good service, and
attended the motion both of horse and foot. After
a desperate conflict, in which the musqueteers played
hard on both sides, we retired into the town.

"Tuesday, August 8.—A letter was brought in safely
through the enemy's leaguer from Sir Marmaduke
Langdale to Sir Charles Lucas :—

"'SIR,

"'Your gallantry in resolution and action
during that fierce and furious siege of Colchester
hath already confirmed in us that noble opinion
which we ever retained of you in all your undertakings
both for spirit and knowledge. Valour acquits itself
best in extreames. Of this your loyall prowesse hath
given ample testimony. . . . . These men's
designs who push at nothing but crowns may afford
both you and me, who stand in defence of a just
cause, and no private interest (as God is our witnesse),
this useful lesson, rather to sacrifice our lives to a

H

noble and memorable fate than to submit to an imperious and mercilesse foe.

" 'Hold on, brave sir; continue your resolution, pursue your sallies, let not their numerous recruits amaze you. Give me leave, for the true zeal I bear to your cause and love to your person, to inforce this needless advice. . . . . . Now, to enliven the hopes of all that brave and honourable cavalry there with you, think every evening how we are one day's march nearer you than we were in the morning, and that our heartiest wishes go along with you, as we are very confident within a few daies with our hands to assist you. . . . . Dear sir, hold out but a little, a very little space; your friends will visit you, and bring you off with honour, and with joyful embraces congratulate you for making loyalty your object of valour.

" ' Sir, your most constant servant,

"' M. L.'

"Wednesday, August 9.—Now began horse-flesh to be more precious to our starving men than the choicest viands had been formerly. All from the lords to the humblest soldier eat nothing else of animal food, unlesse it were cats and dogs. These were killed the first, that they might not prey on the rats and mice, which were reserved for the poorer

people. And so great was the universal necessity
that the horses were no longer secure in the stables,
some being purloined and knocked on the head every
night, and afterwards sold by the pound in the
shambles.* Nor in a short time was there a dog left
in the place, it being a custom with the soldiers to
save a part of their scanty allowance of bread, and
with a morsel of it entice any dog they could discover
in the streets till it came within reach, and then,
killing it with the butt end of their musquets, they
carried it off to their quarters. Six shillings were
known to be given for the side of a dog, and even
that a small one. Still the resolution of the garrison
is unconquerable.

"Thursday, August 10.—An affecting incident
occurred to-day. The Governor, the Earl of Norwich
(the Lady Norwich being newly dead), received a
visit from his daughter, the Lady Catherine Scott.
This lady, attended by Lady Stapylton, obtained
permission from the Lord Generall to pass his lines
upon condition that she did not go into the town.
Lord Norwich met and conversed with her for two
hours outside the sally port in Head Gate. It was
to all appearance a most painful interview. Lady
Catherine Scott was accompanied by Quartermaster

* 780 horses were given in by the commissary as killed by him, besides those stolen by the soldiers, and those the gentlemen had slain for
their own use.—" Carter's True Relation of Siege."

H 2

Gravener, Captain Denison, with Ensign Tower and a guard of soldiers. These we entertained with a collation of horse-flesh stewed in claret, and a bottle or two of wine, the best accommodation we could treat them with, which they ate heartily and liked.

"Friday, August 11.—No present intention to surrender. This morning we set a windmill to work, which we have lately formed on the top of the castle. The enemy perceiving it made shott at the sayles from the New Fort, near Magdalen Church. Two shotts struck it, so that it is made unuseful for the present.

"An order is given out that the men should be careful, and not waste their powder by firing without great occasion, and that no gunner should fire a cannon without the command of a field officer of his post or a general officer of the field. The houses under the wall in East Street, and between St. Botolph and the East Gate, proved so advantageous to the enemy in firing upon our line that our officers, knowing no surer remedy, sallied out amongst them, and beat them out of the streets, and fired the houses. In many places the stairs of these houses came up to the top of our wall in the highest parts of it, some of them being so wide that two or three men might come up abreast; even some of the rooms are on a level with our platforms.

"Saturday, August 12.—There is a tumultuous assemblage of the populace. A clamoursome crowd of famine-stricken people besiege the Lord Governor's quarters, demanding either bread or a surrender. The women and children in particular throw themselves on the ground before the guard, with frantic cries for food.

" Sunday, August 13.—The health of the garrison is much affected. The soldiers suffer from the bloody flux. We give them puddings made of sugar, starch, and currants, and this is found an efficient antidote.

"Monday, August 14.—Our men sallied out at East Gate, and drove from their entrenchments a party of the Suffolk forces, who had brought their galleries within a musquet-shot of the walls. At the same time a sortie was made out of St. Botolph's Gate by the Kentish men, who had a sharp encounter with Colonel Barkstead's foot. The soldiers came to push of pikes, and our scythemen gored and mangled many of their foes before they retired to the walls.

" Tuesday, August 15.—A Council of War is held in the General Fairfax's quarters, at which it is reported by our scouts that a storming of the town is really determined on. Five men, three being horsemen, swam across the river, and decamped to the enemy.

"Wednesday, August 16.—There is great suffering

in the town. A woman, the mother of five children, having her infant at her breast and her other children around her, went out of the town, and beseeched the enemy's sentinels to let her pass beyond their line. Many other women with their families were watching her from the walls and houses; but on observing that she was brought back by a guard of soldiers the crowd slowly broke up, and returned to their sorrowful habitations.

" Thursday, August 17.—Our Council of War refuses to sanction the exchange of the Earl of Cleveland for any of the Committee. This evening one of our master-gunners took an aim at General Fairfax while examining a fort near East Gate. The shot scattered dust upon him and his attendants, injuring one of them by the rebound of a stone; and a matrose was killed while looking over the wall.

"Friday, August 18.—A terrible proof is given this day of the extreme scarcity of food existing in our lines. A horse of one of the enemy's troopers was shot dead. A party of our men rushed out to drag his body within the gate, but not succeeding in the attempt they adventured their lives a second time to cut pieces off, some being slain by the carcase.

"Saturday, August 19.—Lord Norwich and his Council of War send a warrant to the constables of each parish in the town to require all persons and families who have not the means of subsistence for twenty days to leave the town. The municipal authorities wait on the Governor and obtain his permission that they may communicate with Sir Thomas Fairfax, and obtain his leave for the inhabitants to pass through his lines. The Mayor sends a letter to the General by a trumpeter, who also bears a communication from Lord Norwich concerning the exchange of Captain Gray for Mr. Weston and Mr. Rawlins, and concerning the surrender of the town on certain conditions.

" Sunday, August 20.—Sir Thomas Fairfax agrees to the proposed exchange of prisoners, and expresses his willingness to grant a pass to the inhabitants, if the Parliament's Committee be allowed to go out with them.

" Monday, August 21.—Lord Norwich orders a strict domiciliary visit to all the houses in the town in search of food for his soldiers. Private stores are ransacked, and those families that are found to have provisions are allowed a peck of flour for daily use, the rest being taken for the garrison; yet the supply for the soldiers is exceedingly small.

" Tuesday, August 22.—Lord Norwich, Lord Capel, and Sir Charles Lucas again write to General Fairfax, and declare their intention of compelling the towns-

people to leave the town.   Some women and children
go out, and try to pass through the Suffolk forces
near the North Gate, but are compelled by the guards
of the Tower regiment, under Colonel Rainsborough,
to return.

"Wednesday, August 23.—The Mayor and municipal authorities send Dr. Glisson, a physician in the
town, to press on Sir Thomas Fairfax a request for
the inhabitants to have a free pass through his camp.
The appeal is unsuccessful, and Lord Norwich with-
draws his order for their compulsory expulsion.
Another negotiation is commenced with General
Fairfax.   The members of the Parliament's Committee deem the time is come at which they may
again discharge the part of mediators.   They send,
with the sanction of Lord Norwich, Major Samuel
Sheffield to the General's quarters to persuade him
to consent to a treaty with the defenders of the town.
Our troopers sign this day a protest, by which they
pledge themselves not to desert each other or the
foot-soldiers until they have forced a passage through
the enemies' quarters, and to accept of no terms by
which their liberties may be infringed or their honours
blemished.   Rumours begin to prevail of the defeat
and ruin of the Duke of Hamilton's army.   General
Fairfax yet carries on the operations of the siege.
Four great cannon have played this day from the new

fort erected near Magdalen Church, and have done injury to the Priory at St. Botolph's.

"Thursday, August 24.—The news of the total defeat of the Scots' army is confirmed. A kite, bearing in its tail a report of the fight and victory, is sent into the town. The enemy fired three times a volley along their whole line in token of rejoicing. Our commanders summon a council, and send a letter to Fairfax stating the lowest terms on which they will surrender the town. They consent to deliver up all the magazines, arms, ammunition, and stores of war, but demand that the whole garrison, officers and men, may march for one mile out of the town with military honour, and then have a free pass to their own homes or to foreign parts. The Parliament's Committee send out one of their number, Mr. Barnardiston, to entreat of Fairfax an agreement to these terms. The soldiers on both sides continue during those preliminary negotiations the conduct of the siege. A mine at East Gate is this day counter-mined by our men, and the five men working in it are taken prisoners, and brought into the town.

"Friday, August 25.—General Fairfax is inexorable, and refuses to accept the ultimatum of our Council of War. He has sent this letter to our generals :—

" ' MY LORDS,

" ' When I looked upon your condition to be far better than now it is, I then offered terms as was thought suitable to your condition; but you now being in a worse posture, both in relation to your- selves within, and in relation to any expectance of relief from without, it is not to be expected from me that your conditions should be better. Wherefore I am still resolved not to grant any such terms as are now demanded by you.

" ' Your Lordships' servant,

" ' THOS. FAIRFAX.

" ' *The Hyth, Aug. 25th.*'

" On these tidings being made known it was resolved that at nightfall there should be a general simultaneous attempt made from all the gates to attack the enemy, and to force a passage through their quarters. Our officers, to encourage the soldiers and to show their determination to share their fate, and to have a common lot in a like perilous under- taking, divide with them the remaining provisions, and supply them with burnt raisins, sack, and claret. At the last moment this bold design is abandoned. Whether promoted by intrigue from without or by

treachery from within, an unaccountable panic suddenly spread among the men. They who through
this long interval had borne without a murmur the
extremity of privation, and who had manifested an
enthusiastic attachment to their leaders, in this last
moment of trial, entertain the most unworthy suspicions, and yield a blind credence to imputations on
their leaders which none but an enemy, animated by
the worst motives, could have published or invented.
An universal distrust succeeds to the former universal
confidence. All is panic, confusion, invective, and
recrimination.

" Saturday, August 26.—All is lost but honour.
At twelve o'clock Mr. Barnardiston and Colonel Tuke
are sent to the head-quarters of the General, with
instructions to negotiate a treaty, and to endeavour to
obtain for the besieged a favourable interpretation of
the term 'surrendering to mercy.' They do not
return to the town till after eight o'clock in the
evening, and then relate that they have failed in
obtaining from General Fairfax any relaxation of the
terms insisted on in his previous communications.
The Royalist leaders hold a council, the result of
which is a determination to make an unconditional
surrender of the town.*

* " Articles agreed upon the 27th of August, 1648, by and between the
Commissioners of his Excellency the Lord Generall Fairfax on the one
part, and the Commissioners of the Earl of Norwich, Lord Capell, and

" Sunday, August 27.—*Dies nefastus et infandus.*
The commanders at an early hour send the Parliament's Committee to the camp of General Fairfax,
and with them the following letter :—

" ' MY LORD,

" ' Having hitherto acted the duty of soldiers
and gentlemen, we must acknowledge the truth of

Sir Charles Lucas on the other part, for and concerning the rendition of
the town and garrison of Colchester.

" 1. That all the horses belonging to the officers, souldiers, and gentlemen engaged in Colchester, with saddles and bridles to them, shall be
brought into Marie's Churchyard by 9 of the clock to-morrow morning,
and the spare bridles and saddles into that church, and delivered without wilful spoyle to such as the Lord General shall appointe to take
charge of them.

" 2. That all the arms, colours, and drums belonging to any of the
persons in Colchester above mentioned, shall be brought into St. James'
Church by x of the clock to-morrow morning, and delivered, without
wilful spoyle or embesselment to such as the Lord General shall
appoint to take charge of them.

" 3. That all private soldiers and officers under captains shall be drawne
together into the Fryers' Yard, adjoining to the East Gate, by x of the
clock to-morrow, with their cloathes and baggage, their persons to be
rendered into the custody of such as the Lord Generall shall appoint to
take charge of them, and that they shall have fayre quarter, according
to the explanation made in the answer to the first case of the Commissioners from Colchester.

" 4. That the Lords and all captains and superior officers and gentlemen of quality ingaged in Colchester, shall be drawne together there to
the King's Head, with their clothes and baggage, by xi of the clock to-
morrow and there render themselves to the mercy of the Lord Generall
into the hands of such as he shall appoint to take charge of them, and
that a list of all the generall officers and field officers now in command
in the towne be sent to the Lord Generall by ix of the clock in the
morning.

" 5. That all guards within the town of Colchester shall be withdrawn

what is intimated by your Lordship, that there is a great alteration* between our condition and yours since the first overture of a treaty; wherefore, according to your Lordship's admission, we have

---

from the lines, forts, and other places by viii of the clock to-morrow morning, and such as the Lord Generall shall appoint shall thereupon come in to their roomes.

" 6. That all the ammunition shall be preserved in the places where it lyes, to be delivered to the comptroller of his Excellency's traine, by x of the clock to-morrow morning, and all waggons belonging to the souldiers, or persons engaged, with the harnesse belonging thereunto, shall be brought to some convenient place near the ammunition to be delivered to the same person by the same hours.

" 7. That such as are wounded and sicke in the towne shall be there kept and provided for, with accommodation requisite for men in their condition, and not removed thence until they be recovered, or able without prejudice to their healthe to remove, and shall have chyrurgeons to look to them as are now in the town.

" 8. That all ordnance in the towne, with their appurtenances, shall without wilful spoyle, be left at the several platformes or places where they are now planted, and so delivered to his Excellencie's guard that shall take the charge of those places respectively.

" 9. That from henceforth there shall be a cessation of arms on both parts, but the forces within the town to keep their own guards, and the Lord Generall's to keep theirs, until they be removed according to the articles aforesaid.

" Signed by us,

" THOS. HONEYWOOD,	BRUM. GURDON,	WILLIAM COMPTON,
" H. IRETON,	I. SPARROW,	AB. SHIPMAN,
" THOS. RAINSBOROUGH,	ISAAC EWER,	EDW. HAMMOND,
" EDWARD WHALLEY,	THOS. COOKE,	S. TUKE,
" WILL. BLOYS,	G. BARNARDISTON,	WM. AYLIFFE."

* There were only three barrels of powder left, and all the provisions were exhausted. All expectation of external help had failed. Such was the great alteration in their condition referred to by the Royalist leaders.

sent Sir William Compton, Sir Abraham Shipman, Colonel Hamond, Colonel Tuke, and Colonel Ayloffe, to treat and conclude upon the circumstances necessary for the clearing and orderly performance of that which your Lordship in your last hath offered, we being resolved to commit ourselves your Lordship's prisoners.

> " ' Your servants,
>
> > " ' NORWICH.   ARTHUR CAPEL.
> > " ' CHARLES LUCAS.

" ' *Colchester, Aug.* 27*th,* 1648.

" ' According to your Lordship's desire, we have sent you the Committee.' "

Such was the final termination of this protracted and momentous siege, continued in the face of such unequal odds through the long summer days and nights of June, July, and August, 1648.   Commenced by men of lofty principles and noble aspirations, in the hope of restoring peace to a distracted kingdom by the restoration of the captive monarch, Charles I., to his throne, its patient sufferings and active heroisms accomplished nothing beyond the benefit to all generations of a good example of virtuous patriotism and magnanimous self-sacrifice.

Concluded with irremediable disaster, and accompanied by the almost simultaneous defeat of the Duke of Hamilton's Scottish army, the efforts of the Royalists for the deliverance of the King were proved to be impotent and unavailing.

Within four months of the surrender of Colchester, on the re-assembling of Fairfax's army in London, the party in the Parliament hostile to the monarchy drove out from the House of Commons by a *coup d'état* (known in history as Colonel Pride's Purge, from his active superintendence and agency in the transaction) their more scrupulous colleagues, and proceeded at once to carry out their foredetermined plans of bringing their sovereign to a public trial, and to a death upon the scaffold. It is not to be wondered, that those who were at this very time contemplating and discussing in their camp-circles the perpetration of these extreme and ruthless councils against the life and person of their King, should also be found to forewarn him of his impending fate, by their inflicting the penalty of death upon his faithful, true, and loyal champions, the brave defenders in his name of the town of Colchester.

CHAPTER VIII.

THE MORROW OF THE SURRENDER.

" The glories of our birth and state
   Are shadows, not substantial things;
There is no armour against fate,
   Death lays his icy hands on kings;
     Sceptre and crown
     Must tumble down,
And in the dust be equal made
With the poor crooked scythe and spade."

                    SHIRLEY

Arrangements for the cession of the town—Places assigned for the surrender of horses, arms, officers, and lords—Escape of Colonel Farre—
Triumphal entry of Sir Thomas Fairfax—His success not an unalloyed
satisfaction—Council and discussion at the Moot Hall—The condemnation of three knights—A solemn farewell—Woe to the conquered—
Vain efforts of the Lords—The last speeches, prayers, and execution
of Sir Charles Lucas—The brave bearing and death of Sir George
Lisle—Reprieve of Sir Bernard Gascoigne—The general condemnation of the execution—Honours to the Royalist sufferers.

THE town of Colchester, on the " morrow of the surrender," presented a great contrast to the scenes
enacted within its walls during the preceding twelve
weeks. There was no longer the clang of martial
music, the boom of the cannon, the challenge of the
sentinel, the shout of the combat, the cheerful tramp
of resolute, suffering, but unconquered men. The
réveille indeed sounded as usual at break of day, but

the rolls of its drums announced the preparations for the painful events that day to be transacted. The soldiers and officers, with downcast looks, subdued voices, and aching hearts, yet with the inward consciousness of parts well played, and of fame well earned, faithfully carried out the conditions to which they were engaged. At eight o'clock in the morning of Monday, August 28th, all the guards were withdrawn from the whole circuit of the walls. The Church of St. Mary's, the witness throughout the siege of the triumphant resistance of the Royalists and the site of their strongest and best furnished fort, was now chosen as the scene of their humiliation. All the surviving horses of officers and of troopers in the cavalry (reported to be 120 in number), equipped in their military saddles, bridles, and accoutrements, were ordered to be assembled in the churchyard of St. Mary's by nine o'clock. The spare saddles, bridles, and ornaments were collected in heaps within the church. The foot soldiers were directed to deposit their arms, drums, and colours in the Church of St. James, adjoining East Gate, by ten o'clock. The soldiers themselves, at the same hour, were marched without their arms, but with their clothes and baggage, into the Fryar's Yard, East Gate, to await the entrance of their conquerors.

The Lords Norwich, Loughborough, and Capel,

I

with Sir Charles Lucas, Sir George Lisle, Sir Bernard
Gascoigne, with all the gentlemen and officers
above the rank of captain, were commanded to surrender themselves at the " King's Head " * at eleven
o'clock. In spite of the darkly hinted threats of
vengeance uttered by Sir Thomas Fairfax and his
council of war in the progress of the preceding negotiations, no one absented himself, nor attempted to
escape, with the exception of Colonel Farre,† who hid
himself in the town, hopeless of mercy by the express
exemption from the terms of surrender of all those
who had deserted from the army of the Parliament
since the preceding month of May.‡

* The King's Head was the chief inn. It stood in Head Street, near
the Head Gate. The houses in " Observatory Court" formed part of
this ancient hostelry. This property is identified by the description
given of it in the deeds of transfer held by the head-master of the
Royal Grammar School in Colchester.

† Colonel Farre hid himself in a cellar, but was discovered, and
taken prisoner. By order of the Parliament he was committed for
trial by Sir Thomas Fairfax, whose council of war condemned him to
be shot.

‡ List of the prisoners who delivered themselves upon the surrender
of Colchester, Aug. 28, 1648 :—

The Earl of Norwich, Commander-in-Chief.

LORDS AND GENTLEMEN.

Lord Capell,	Sir John Watts,	Sir Dennard Strutt,
Lord Loughborough,	Sir Lodowick Dyer,	Sir Hugh Oriley,
Sir Bernard Gascoyn,	Sir Henry Appleton,	Sir Rich. Maulyverer.
Sir Abr. Shipman,		

At 10 o'clock the Tower regiment, under Colonel Rainsborough, entered the town by the North Gate, and Colonel Ingoldsby's regiment by the Head Gate, in accordance with the treaty of surrender. Four hours later, at two o'clock in the afternoon, the ap-

List of prisoners—*continued.*

COLONELS.

Sir William Compton,	Chester,	Tuke,
Gilbourne,	Till,	Ayloffe,
Farre,	Heath,	Sawyer.
Hammond,		

LIEUTENANT-COLONELS.

Culpepper,	Powell,	Wiseman,
Lancaster,	Ashton,	Smith.
Gough,	Bagley,	

MAJORS.

Amscott,	Ward,	Scarrow,
Smith,	Bayley,	Blyncourt,
Armstrong,	Neale,	Glennings.

CAPTAINS.

Sir Charles Lucas,	Lovell,	Hernor,
Sir George Lisle,	Cooper,	Smith,
Willis,	Blunt,	Kennington
Pitt,	Snellgrove,	Heath,
Bully,	Dynors,	Newton,
Burdge,	Duffrin,	Bailey,
Barthorpe,	Goring,	Stephen,
Linsey,	Ward,	Lodge,
Myldmay,	Buskey,	Lynn,
Osbandeston,	Pain,	White.
Estwich,		

proach of Fairfax himself, from his head-quarters at
the Hyth, into the town was heralded by strains of
military music. A regiment of foot-guards marched
at the head, and another at the rear of the procession.
The General himself was in the centre, surrounded by
a brilliant staff, and accompanied by the varied ranks
of his numerous cavalry. On his reaching East
Gate he found the Mayor and Aldermen awaiting his
arrival. Cries of welcome and congratulation arose
from the populace collected on all sides; and yet that
hour of triumph could not have been accompanied
with feelings of unalloyed satisfaction. Our own
great conqueror, whose name to the elder part of this
generation is and ever will be familiar as a household
word, is reported to have said to a lady congratulat-

List of prisoners—*continued.*

> Lieutenants, Goring, White.
> Edward Goodyeare, Master-General.
> Trowley, Commissary-General.
> Francis Loveless, Master of the Ordnance.
> Matthew Carter, Quarter-Master General.
> Graviston, Waggon-Master General.

Servants attending Lords and Gentlemen	65
Lieutenants	73
Ensigns and Cornets	69
Sergeants	183
Rank and File	3,067

Total, including Lords and Gentlemen........ 3,530

" Carter's True Relation," p. 76.

ing him on his success at Waterloo : " Madam, the greatest misfortune that can happen to a man, next to losing a battle, is to win one." If this be true of a victory gained over foreign foemen, how much more poignant must be the sorrow attendant on a triumph over fellow-countrymen and fellow-citizens, brothers in blood, language, and religion. Fairfax, amidst all his failings, was a humane man, and he could not on this occasion have seen, as he ascended the hill of East Street,* the fair and stately houses wrecked, ruined, and destroyed by fire, nor have looked as he passed on the groups of unarmed, half-starved men, collected in the Grey-fryars, nor have viewed the gaunt forms and famished † countenances of the shouting crowd, nor regarded the wrecked and ruined houses, shattered walls, and battered ramparts of the

---

* " It was a sad spectacle to see so many fair houses burnt to ashes, and so many inhabitants made so weak with living upon horses and dogs. The town had suffered as well as the men, being ruined in its buildings, provisions, people, and trade. What faire streets are here of stately houses now laid in ashes. How eminent are their granaries of corne (which before the enemy came exceeded all parts of England), and their cellars, and storehouses of wine and fruit, where there was plenty before are empty now. They who had houses to live in now live desolate for want of habitation ; and those who had formerly their tables furnished with variety of dishes (besides their usual dainties of oysters and Ringo nuts) have for a long time fed upon horses, dogs, and cats, starch, bran, and graine, and that with much greediness, many starved to death with hunger."—News-Book.

† " Death was written in many of their countenances, yet did many of these loyally affected spirits smile at their sufferings, as if the goodness of their cause had fortified them against all miseries."—News-Book.

gateway frowning above his head, without some sentiments of regret, and sympathy for the sufferings,
miseries, and sorrows consequent on the strife in
which he was engaged.

Fairfax proceeded, however, on his route, and dismounted at the ancient Moot Hall (which then stood
in the centre of High Street) at about three o'clock in
the afternoon. He immediately summoned his officers,
and held a council of war in the large chamber of the
Hall, at which the fate of the leaders of the Royalists
was to be decided on. A short but spirited discussion ensued, in which much diversity of opinion was
expressed. Colonel Whalley, who had distinguished
himself greatly by his gallantry during the operations
of the siege, advocated the adoption of a lenient and
merciful course. General Ireton, on the contrary,
in vehement language demanded the lives of the
chief leaders of the surrendered army. Fairfax was
irresolute.* " Revenge pricked him on. Honour
drew him off." As in all such cases the firm and
resolute prevailed over the vacillating and uncertain.
Sentence was given in accordance with the most
violent counsels. It was decreed that four of the
commanders, Sir Charles Lucas, Sir George Lisle,

* Some say Fairfax never forgave Sir Charles Lucas the repulse received from him at Marston Moor ; but this is too paltry a motive to
have weighed with Fairfax on this momentous occasion.

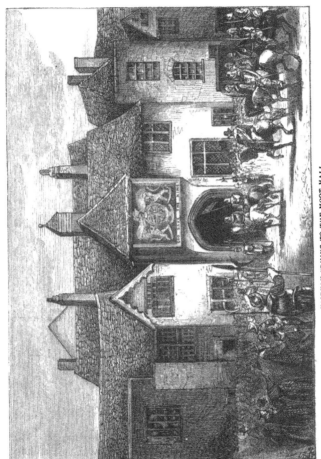

FAIRFAX COMING TO THE MOOT HALL.

Siege of Colchester, page 118.

Sir Bernard Gascoigne, and Colonel Farre, should be
led to immediate execution; and that Lords Norwich,
Loughborough, and Capel should be detained as
State prisoners, until the pleasure of Parliament in
regard to them could be known.   In accordance with
this decision, shortly before four o'clock, Colonel Ewers
was sent to summon the condemned leaders to the
presence of the council.   Proceeding to the "King's
Head," he entered the room within which the Royalist officers and gentlemen were guarded, and with
words of scant courtesy required the instant attend-
ance of the three doomed knights at the Moot Hall.
With a sad and sure prescience of their coming fate,
they took a hasty but solemn farewell of their companions, and were marched away through Head Street
and High Street under the charge of a company of
foot-guards.   On their admission to the council-
chamber, General Ireton announced to them in abrupt
speech the decision of Fairfax and his officers.   Sir
Charles Lucas, as the spokesman for the others, fear-
lessly inquired by what right they were condemned to
die, and demanded a fair trial according to the laws of
the land.   His remonstrances were in vain.   His companions and himself were obliged to submit to the woe
proverbially the lot of the conquered, and were hurried
away under the protection of a strong guard from the
council-room to the castle.   The petition that they

might be respited till the morning to settle their
affairs was refused. At the same time they were
offered the services of the Lord General's chaplain*
" to advise, comfort, and prepare them before their
end ! " This proposal they declined, but requested
instead the presence of the chaplain of Lord Norwich
(probably a Mr. Harman, who was the Vicar of St.
Mary's and the chief clergyman in the town, and who
had greatly distinguished himself by his zeal and
sympathy with the Royalists during the whole period
of the siege), and with him they passed the short
residue of their time in the participation of the Holy
Communion, and in earnest, devout prayer.

In the meanwhile the Lords Norwich, Loughborough, and Capel, with the rest of the prisoners at
the " King's Head," made a noble effort in behalf of
their friends. On hearing the summons sent to the
chaplain of Lord Norwich, they entreated the presence
of Captain Cannon, the captain of the guard to
whose custody they were assigned, and they prevailed
on him to go in their names to the council, and to
implore General Fairfax that they might be included
in any sentence passed upon their friends ; " as it
was only just," they said, " that as all had been

* Matthew Carter, the Quartermaster of the Royal army, states that
the Rev. Joshua Sprigge, author of " Anglia Rediviva " was Chaplain to
Fairfax during the Siege.—" True Relation," p. 101.

equally guilty in the warfare, so all should bear an equal share in the retribution." These entreaties on behalf of their friends were disregarded. No prayers, arguments, nor remonstrances could change the resolve or soften the anger of their stern and relentless conquerors.

Seven o'clock in the evening was the time named by the council of war for the execution. Precisely as that hour struck, the three condemned knights, Sir Charles Lucas, Sir George Lisle, and Sir Bernard Gascoigne, were marched from the castle to the spot, yet marked with a small stone in the ditch or bailey on the north side of that ancient building. In addition to the guard who attended them, Colonels Whalley and Rainsborough, with General Ireton and three files of musqueteers, were assembled at the place. Sir Charles Lucas was selected to be the first victim. In the act of being moved in front of the firing party he said, " I have often looked death in the face both publique and private, and you shall now see I dare to die." Being placed in position he made an address, according to the established custom of the day.

" Gentlemen souldiers," he said, " as I am a free-born Englishman, I desire that I may have the benefit of the lawes of the land, that I may see my accusers, and plead face to face; and have liberty to put in my answer, and be tryed by indifferent judges. Was it ever knowne that a man did suffer in this kind in cold blood by such an order as this, after a surrender by treaty upon termes of mercy ?   Oh, what mercy there be in death, save only that one kind is not so bitter as another !

"I doe humbly desire this favour (if it may be), that I may have liberty to speak with the Lord Generall, by whose power I am thus condemned to suffer death. I have something which I would impart unto his Excellency, that I hope may give him such satisfaction as may cause this bloody cloud to bee removed from over my head."

To this speech an answer was made by Colonel Rainsborough, against whom Sir Charles Lucas had formerly held Berkeley Castle.

"Sir Charles,

"You have surrendered this garrison upon mercy, which word mercy you desired might be explained, which was accordingly (done) by your commissioners and ours.   The explanation you well know was, that you should be rendered to us with certaine assurance of quarter, so as the Lord Generall may be free to put some immediately to the sword (if wee see cause). And do you now dispute the case against yourself and your owne act ?

" His Excellency (you know) may execute you all (all the chiefe officers among you), and that he saves any itt is mercy.   Now that he causeth you and some few others to be executed, and saves all the rest, how can you call it cruelty ? "

In addition to this reply of Colonel Rainsborough, one of the soldiers was allowed to address Sir Charles Lucas, and to accuse him of cruelty towards the Parliamentarian soldiers on his taking of Froome Castle.

These recriminations and reproaches of a help-less captive in the very moment of a predetermined execution are not to be judged of by the light and experience of our happier days.   With us they would now be the veriest exaggerations of malice, or the cunningest refinements of cruelty.   In the time they occurred they were justified by the strong plea of universal custom, and reflected no discredit on either the hero of the solemn tragedy, or on his vic-torious executioners.

Sir Charles Lucas, however, finding that in this last crisis of his fate all appeal for mercy was in vain, set himself more directly to a preparation for the fatal sentence, and for the second time made an address to the bystanders :

" Good people," he said, " I am now to pay that

debt which we all owe.   Every man must dye—that
is most certaine—but how or when is not tenour to
any.   It is my chance now (though unhappily in
blood); none of you know when it may be any of your
turnes.

"As for my offence, it is, you all know, for main-
taining his Majestie's cause, which hath been according to my judgment, and I believe that I went the
right way, and I am sure I was firm to that cause I
undertook.

"But, seeing I must dye, and that there is no way
to obtaine mercy, but that I must now finish my
course this way, to which I beseech Almighty God to
assist me, to dye with comfort in my Saviour.

"I bequeath my soul into the hands of my Maker,
God the Father, Son, and Holy Ghost, three Persons
and one God.   Oh! doe Thou, my Lord God Almighty
(for my blessed Saviour the Lord Jesus' sake), receive
my soul to eternal glory.

"I have lived a Protestant, and a Protestant here
I dye, in the faith of the Church of England, that
hath beene established so many yeares.   And as for
these souldiers who stand ready to shoot me, I yield
my life to their hands, and I pray God to forgive
them.   I doe freely from my heart forgive them."

Having thus spoken, he knelt down, and prayed

earnestly with himself. The broken words heard to
escape his lips were to this import: "And so to
Thee, O Lord, I commend my soul—Lord Jesus, receive my spirit. Oh, Father, Son, and Holy Ghost,
receive my soul to Thy mercy. Come, Lord Jesus,
receive my soul." After a very brief interval he
stood up with a cheerful and resolved air, every
token of disorder being removed from his countenance,
and pulled his hat firmly on his head, and hastily
opening his doublet, exposed his naked breast to the
firing party, and placing his hands to his side in an
attitude* of defiance he exclaimed, with a sudden and
loud vehemence: "Now, rebels, do your worst." An
instantaneous discharge of musketry was the reply;
and Sir Charles Lucas,† pierced to the heart with
four mortal wounds, fell down dead.

* "He set his arms akimbo, that was his position."—"Loyall Sacrifice," p. 78.

† Sir Charles Lucas is described as "an accomplished soldier, a perfect
master of all the mysteries both of antient and modern militia, and judged
as eminent in command of horse as any in Europe."—"Loyall Sacrifice."
He took an active part in the earlier part of the first civil war. He defended Berkeley Castle against Colonel Rainsborough; rescued Bever-
ston Castle from Massey at the time of the siege of Gloucester, forced
his way through the Parliamentary army at Carwood, and had almost
secured the victory for the Royalists at Marston Moor, giving Fairfax
so rough a handling that he is supposed ever after to have borne a
grudge against him. After the battle of Marston Moor, he is said to
have given his parole to Fairfax not to fight for the King. If this statement be true, the parole could only be supposed to extend to the conflict of the two armies then in the field against each other. When the
Royal army was totally disbanded, after the flight of Charles I. from

The speeches of Sir Charles Lucas, and the replies made to them, had occupied so long a time, that the shades of evening began to fall thickly about the castle ditch and those assembled there. Sir George Lisle was, however, without delay placed at the stone of execution. On approaching the body of his friend, which for the greater despatch had not been removed nor covered, he knelt down and kissed his cheek with the most reverent affection. He then, according to the prevalent custom, made an address, in which he justified the conduct of himself and of his deceased companion. After having knelt a few minutes in private prayer, in which he invoked with much earnestness the name of Jesus, he arose, and taking five gold pieces out of his purse, gave one to his executioners, and desired that the other four might be sent to four friends in London. Then, observing the darkness, and thinking the soldiers were placed at too great a distance to see him distinctly, he requested them to advance near—on which one of them said, "I 'll warrant ye, sir, we 'll hit you." Sir George

---

Oxford, the parole would be at end. It is to be observed that Sir Charles Lucas took no part in the first prolonged contest of the civil war subsequent to the battle of Marston Moor. Sir Charles Lucas was brother-in-law of the Marquis of Newcastle, the Commander-in-chief of the Royal army at Marston Moor, at which crisis he resigned his command, and left the kingdom. The marquis married his sister Margaret Lucas, the future famous and learned Duchess of Newcastle.

Lisle,* smiling, replied, " I have been nearer you,
friend, when you missed me." Kneeling down once
again for a few moments, he remained in earnest devotion, and, rising, cheerfully and resolutely presented
himself with heroic demeanour to his fate. Repeat-
ing with a loud voice the words, " Now then, rebels
and traitors, do your worst "—fire was immediately
given, and the work of death was instantaneously
accomplished.

> " The knights' bones are dust
> And their good swords rust ;
> Their souls are with the saints, we trust." †

This summary vengeance on the Royalist leaders
was an entirely new proceeding, not hitherto sanctioned
by precedent or example. Up to this time the name
of the sovereign was allowed to justify a resort to
arms. The worst penalties exacted from those who
lost the day worsted in the fight were imprisonment,
fines, or the confiscation of estates. The carnage in
cold blood of these two valiant commanders (for Sir

* Sir George Lisle was reputed to have been as excellent in command
of infantry as Sir Charles Lucas was of cavalry. He had such influence
with, and command over his men, that he could lead them as in a string
for any purpose. He distinguished himself during the first civil war
on many occasions by his personal bravery, especially at the battle of
Newbury, in which he put off his armour, even to his buff doublet, and
fought in his shirt alone, that his soldiers might in the dusk better
observe him from whom they were to receive both direction and
courage.

† Coleridge.

Bernard Gascoigne* had been reprieved at the last
moment) shook to its centre the fabric of English
society. The deed was sifted and canvassed on all
sides. It was extenuated by a few as an act of necessity, censured by the vast majority as impolitic, and
condemned by many as a cruel and wilful murder.
It gave rise to a fruitful crop of elegies, epitaphs, addresses, and sermons. The author of one of these
discourses† had the courage to write, in the very
moment of the triumph of the conquering army,
" Wherever loyalty and obedience shall have the reputation of virtues, there shall the names of Lucas and
Lisle be ever honoured : for to omit the honour of
their extraction, the honour of their employments, the
honour of their martial achievements, the honour of
their last sufferings, render them most honourable."

* Sir Bernard Gascoigne was a gentlemen of Florence, who had
served the King in the war, and afterwards remained in London till the
unhappy adventure at Colchester, and then accompanied his friends
thither. He had only English enough to make himself understood that he
desired a pen, ink, and paper, that he might write a letter to his prince,
the great Duke, that his Highness might know in what manner he lost
his life, to the end his heirs might have his estate. . . . . . Sir
Bernard Gascoigne had his doublet off, and expected the next salvo ;
but the officer told him he had orders to carry him back to his friends.
The Council of War had considered that if they resolved in this way take
the life of a foreigner, who seemed to be a person of quality, that their
friends, or children, who should visit Italy, might pay dear for many
generations ; and therefore they commanded the officer, when the other
two were dead, to carry him back to the other prisoners."—Lord
Clarendon's " History of the Rebellion." Book xi., s. 107.

† " Triumph of Loyalty." A sermon, preached Sept. 13, 1648.

CHAPTER IX.

THE PASQUINADES OF THE SIEGE.

" If I lash vice in general fiction,
Is 't I apply, or self-conviction?
I no man call or ape or ass,
'Tis his own conscience holds the glass."

GAY.

" Hearken unto a verser, who may chance
Rhyme thee to good."

SHAKESPEARE.

The origin of weekly newspapers in England—Ballads a means of political strife—Siege of Colchester a fruitful theme for ballad-makers—Examples of ballads on earlier events of siege—Ballads on the protracted continuance of the siege—The sufferings of the besieged described—An elegy on the three Royalist leaders.

THE first publication* of a weekly journal or newspaper in England commenced just anterior to the period of the Commonwealth. The more active promoters of the great Rebellion desired to enflame the popular mind, and to make the masses of their countrymen

* In 1622 Nathaniel Butler published " The News of the Present Week," and in 1626 he continued this under the title of " Mercurius Britannious." In 1641 a Diurnal was published of the occurrences of Parliament. In 1661 Sir Roger L'Estrange commenced the " Public Intelligencer," the first newspaper in the present form.

acquainted with their motives, principles, and intentions, and for the more effectual accomplishment of this purpose they greatly multiplied these weekly messengers and issued frequent addresses and appeals to disseminate news and to promote the interests of their party. A large number of newspapers, Mercuries* with divers names, descriptive of the particular interests they espoused, Flying Kites, Scottish Doves, Moderate Intelligencers, &c., were printed and distributed throughout the towns and counties with a weekly circulation. These publications not only related the actual events that occurred in England, the progress of sieges, the issue of battles, the movements of troops, the proceedings, health, or employments of the King, or described the politics or the ceremonies of foreign courts and camps, but they became the acknowledged channels of the defence and advocacy of the cause they represented, and the surest instrument of antagonism and of mischief to their opponents. One form of this incessant verbal strife and literary warfare was the publication of ribald ballads or of political rythmical effusions. In this later, second civil war, related in this volume, every

* Mercurius Britannicus, Mercurius Rusticus, Mercurius Aulicus, Mercurius Pragmaticus, Mercurius Bellicus, Mercurius Eleucticus, Mercurius Insanus, Mercurius Melancholicus, Mercurius Urbanus, Mercurius Psitacus.

event that transpired became the subject of verse. The
shaft more often hit the mark when clothed with the
satirical inspiration of the poet, than when furnished
only from the pen of the narrator. The rhyme often
proved a barbed arrow, dealing a deadly wound, when
the most earnest address in prose fell harmless on
the foe as the dart of Priam.

" Telum imbelle atque sine ictu."

A contest so evenly balanced and so unexpectedly
protracted as that maintained at Colchester, on which
two such mighty issues depended as the restoration
of the sovereign, or the continued predominance of
the Parliament, and the consequent humiliation of
one party and the elevation of another, was through
the whole of its duration a very harvest to the
chroniclers of the times.   The directors of the
journals, especially of those in the interests of the
Court, entered as keenly into the contest as the
Royalist leaders themselves.   They hailed every
gleam of hope with the fondest expectations of
ultimate success, magnified every favourable circumstance into the largest proportions, vaunted with
enthusiastic encomiums the marvellous pluck and
admirable perseverance of their friends, supported
them in their struggle with words of boldest encour-
agement, and predicted their triumph with premature

K 2

pæans of praise and congratulation. There was scarcely a circumstance, from the very commencement to the very end of the siege, which does not afford a subject for rhyme, and become a theme of poetical effusion. Instead of interrupting his narrative by the chronological insertion of these poetical comments on passing events, the author has preferred to devote a special chapter to these "Pasquinades of the Siege of Colchester."* The reader of the preceding pages will require but few words to illustrate their meaning, or enforce their interpretation.

These following five examples refer to the commencement of the siege, and explain the position of affairs as set forth at length in the successive chapters of this volume :—

I.

"The Prince, the Duke, the bonny Scot,
    The Welsh, the Irish too,
Have for the Roundheads† cast their lot,
    How sudden is their woe."

---

* Pasquinades, so called from an old and mutilated statue in the city of Rome, on which it is the custom to hang lampoons and satirical effusions.

† The name given by the Royalists to their opponents, from their wearing their hair very short.

"Religion in their garments, and their hair
Cut shorter than their eyebrows."
            Prologue to *Every Man out of His Humour.*

II.

1.

' Brave Colchester doth still defy
 The ling'ring saints about it;
Their walls are lyn'd with Loyalty,
 The saints can live without it.

2.

" The fleet are justling to the shoare—
 The highborne Prince of Wales
Is now resolved to try once more
 If he can turn the scales.

3.

" Th' enrag'd Scots have told us now
 What they doe come about,
It is to make the members bowe,
 And put the saints to rout.

4.

" To bring King Charles from th' Isle of Wight,
 And set him on his throne,
To settle Peace, and Truth, and Right,
 Such is the Scottish tone."

III.

" Hye, Hye, dispatch at Colchester,
 And to the North make haste,
Where the Philistine Scots appear
 To lay your Israel waste.
Kiss, kiss the Son before he frown,
 By the treating with your master,
He 's kind, and though you have crackt his crown,
 He must give you a plaister."

IV.

" Blush, England, blush, when the false Scots shall be
More loyal to their sovereign than thee !"

———— ————

V.

" Oh ! let 's not neuters be ! joine heart and hand
  To ease poor England of her native foes,
And turn them headlong to some other land ;
  June cannot end without their overthrows ;
We can't be happy, without all consent
  To have an old King, and new Parliament."

The next series of ballads was written during the
protracted continuance of the siege. The hopes or
the fears of all England were concentrated on the
events transacted at Colchester. The journalist
exhibits the intensest satisfaction in setting before
his readers the supposed evil plight of the Parliamentarian army, and predicts the ruin and failure of
its leaders. The verses are somewhat rough and
scurrilous, but are of value as attesting the character
of the feelings and sentiments contemporaneous
with the events themselves.

I.

1.

" The Essex men have vow'd they will
  Not do their work by halves ;
They have knock'd, and they mean to knock
  The rebells down like calves.

2

" Noll is defunct ; Tom is disjunct ;
  The saints and army shattered ;
Even so it was, God did arise,
  His enemies are scatter'd.

3.

" The King shall have his own againe,
  The kingdome shall be quiet,
And traitors who feed high and fat,
  Must have more moderate diet."

II.

" Shrink not brave heros, be not you dismaid,
Because so long you wast your hoped aid ;
You know it is not easie to bring downe
Traytors, who sit at helme, and grasp a crowne.
The Scots must force their way through Lambert's heart,
And send ten thousand for to claime their part
Amongst the Furies, ere they can come on
With winged haste to your redemption.
The Prince of Wales, although King of the Seas,
Yet feares his cure may add to their disease,
Should he act rashly, and a battaile trie
Ere things are come unto maturitie ;
Things work a-pace. Be patient, and ere long
Unto your rescue come three armies strong."

III.

1.

" The highest floods have lowest ebbs,
  Haste clyming heaviest fall,
Men's councils are but spider webbs,
  One frown of fate spoiles all.

The soaring cedar, forest brusht,
   When sturdy winds do whistle;
The cruel'st creatures* all are husht,
   When angry Lyons† bristle.

2.

" Doe you not hear Heaven's axles crack,
   As if they 'd fall assunder ?
From north to south the raging Rack
   Rides in a range of thunder.
Me thinks I see th' eclypsed sun,‡
   From the sad solstice rise,
Puts out those starres § hath him undone,
   But chears all loyal eyes."

IV.

" In a most sick and weak estate,
   Tom and his army lie ;
But 'tis a strong and powerful fate
   That notes their misery.
Had they but so much light to see
   As Cromwell's snout affords,
They would repent, and converts be
   To Prayers, and not to Swords."

V.

" Yet Colchester bears bravely up,
   They eat and drink apace ;
Lately they gave a deadly cup
   Unto the babes of grace.
Though the saints hope to starve them out,
   Alas ! it nere will be,
For if they grapple t'other bout,
   O Fairfax, farewell thee."

---

* Parliament.   † The Scottish army.
‡ The King.   § The Parliament.

The "deadly cup" of this ballad is the severe
handling of the Sussex forces referred to in the sixth
chapter of this history, in the conflict of July 5th,
in the neighbourhood of the East Gate.   The
journalists in the Royal interests retain their tone
of confidence even unto the last.   They confess in
the next collection of ballads to the privations of
the besieged, but at the same time draw from the
fact of their resorting to horse-flesh for provision
omens of success and topics of consolation.

I.

1.

"Yet Colchester, that loyal town,
    Most daringly out-braves it,
They know 'tis to regain a crown,
    And fight as all should have it.

2.

"What if on horse-flesh they did feed,
    At which the saints might glory;
Yet have they strength to make them bleed,
    That adds unto the story.

3.

I smile to think how cold they stand,
    Now shivering in thinne fleeces,
Who but to warm one bloody hand
    Would rent the land in pieces."

II.

> " Whatever they do eat or drink
>   Breeds loyal blood, no question ;
>   But Fairfax, that hath sweeter meat,
>   Finds but a cold digestion."

III.

> " Hold out then stiffly, Colchester, and be
>   A miracle to all posteritie."

The severe and summary vengeance and unexpected requitals demanded of the Royalists in the immediate execution of their famous leaders, Sir Charles Lucas, Sir George Lisle, and Lord Arthur Capel, naturally excited the utmost indignation of their friends. This indignation found expression in numerous elegies and inscriptions. The two following examples will suffice :—

I.

> " For this High Court of Rebels hath decreed,
>   That whosoever loves their King shall bleed."

II.

> Rome's three Horatii are posed. Our isle
> Hath bred a Capel, Lucas, and a Lisle,
> Whose matchless deeds have dub'd them with that late
> And glorious title of Triumvirate.
> Yet if they expect a shrine on earth, wee must
> Make Colchester th' exchequer of their dust."

CHAPTER X.

THE FURTHER PROCEEDINGS OF FAIRFAX.

> . . . . " The matrons flung their gloves,
> Ladies and maids their scarfs and handkerchiefs,
> Upon him as he passed : the commons made
> A shower and thunder with their caps and shouts ;
> I never saw the like."
>
> SHAKESPEARE.

An imposition on town of Colchester—By whom paid—Receipts for same—How disbursed—Review on Lexden Heath—Dismissal of country forces—Day of public thanksgiving—Sermon by Mr. Owen —" Slighting" of the walls—Movement of the Parliamentarian army —Grand reception of General Fairfax—Treatment of the Royalist soldiers and officers—Inquiry into the conduct of Sir Thomas Fairfax —His account of his council of war—Motives animating the leaders of his army—Their hatred of the King—The true solution of the conduct of Fairfax.

THE town of Colchester soon experienced in its turn the heavy hand of the conqueror. Fairfax and his council of war imposed a fine of twelve thousand pounds upon the inhabitants, in spite of the pro- testation of the mayor and aldermen of their inability to pay, on account of the " miserable, decayed, wasted condition of the town." The late severe and arbitrary treatment of the Royalist leaders so impressed the

townspeople with a salutary fear of offending the
potent and unscrupulous tribunal of the General and
his officers, that, content with a verbal remonstrance,
they at once exerted themselves to the utmost to
satisfy the demands made on them. The Dutch
company of the Bays and Says-makers paid one full
moiety of the whole subsidy required. The other
moiety was made up by the payments of the inhabitants. Some of the receipts of these payments are yet
shown in the museum of the Castle.

COLCHESTER.   August 30th, 1648.

Recd. then by virtue of a warrant from his Excy.
Tho. Ffairfax, bearing date ye 29th instant, of
John Rebow, the sum of fourscore pounds,   xx£
being in /ct of ye Ten Thousand Pounds agreed   ――
to be pd. by the Town of Colchester upon ye   iiij.
reddition of it, as a gratuity to the soldiers.

I say recd.

By me,

JOHN BLACKWELL.

Of this imposition on the town of Colchester £2,000
was remitted to the poorer inhabitants. The records
of the corporation contain a list of those excused*
from payment of their quota, on account of their
houses having been burnt in the siege. The sum of
£8,000 was allotted to the soldiers of the standing

* This explains the item of £10,000 only being mentioned in the
receipt for Mr. Rebow's payment of £80.

army. The remaining £2,000 was divided among
the county forces, the train-bands and yeomanry
cavalry regiments of Essex and Suffolk. The local
troops were in the utmost haste to be dismissed to
their homes. They were composed for the most part
of agricultural labourers, or of mechanics from the
towns, and officered by their neighbours, county
magistrates and squires. The three months spent in
the tented field before the walls of Colchester must
have been to many among them a source of serious
inconvenience, as removing them from their families, their farms, trades, and ordinary occupations.
Sir Thomas Fairfax approved of their immediate
departure, but determined to dismiss them with
military honours. He had already spoken of their
conduct with much eulogy in his official despatch to
the Parliament on the successful issue of the siege,
and now he resolved to prove his personal gratitude
and his high appreciation of their services by dis-
missing them to their homes in the presence of his
whole army. For this purpose he gave orders for a
grand review of all his forces to be held on Lexden
Heath, on Wednesday, the 30th of August, at the
conclusion of which the country regiments were to
march away for their homes amidst the congratu-
lations of their fellow-soldiers. The day proved to
be very wet, and so the ceremony of leave-taking was

interfered with; but the chronicler relates : " Though
the compliment was hindered, yet we shook hands
with them, great volleys of shot past, and they were
dismist."

Fairfax had other duties to attend to before he
took his own departure. The temper of the times,
combined with the general sentiments prevalent
among his soldiers, and with his own personal feelings, induced him to regard his effectual though late
success at Colchester as a special instance of Divine
mercy.   He sets apart, therefore, Thursday, the last
day of August, as a day of public thanksgiving to be
observed with all solemnity by himself and by his
whole army.   The Reverend John Owen was invited
to preach on the occasion.   His sermon, entitled
" Ebenezer,"* a memorial of the deliverance of
Essex, is yet extant.   His text was the third chapter
of Habakkuk, and the first ten verses.   The discourse is remarkable for its verboseness and prolixity.
It gives no information about, or contains scarcely
any allusion to the siege.   Its preface is interesting,
as written in praise of Fairfax, to whose personal
courage in exposing his life in the field he bears
honourable witness.   " Even the life," he says, " of
the meanest soldier in your army was not in more
imminent danger than was oftentimes your own."

* " Ebenezer."   London : Printed by W. Wilson, 1648.

The next important matter that occupied Fairfax's attention was the " slighting," as it was called, or the dismantling the walls and fortifications of the town. The visitor to Colchester will be surprised to find no trace of gate or gateway, barbican or tower, and comparatively meagre portions of the ancient walls. The conduct of Fairfax will in part account for the absence of these ornaments, yet to be found at York, Chester, Hereford, and other formerly walled towns. On the morning of Friday, September 1st, five hundred labourers supplied by the mayor, at the command of Fairfax, were set to work with spades, pickaxes, and hatchets, not only to remove the earthworks and platforms erected by the Royalists for their artillery, but to dismantle or " slight " the walls, to widen the breaches, and to do as much as possible in the way of mischief and destruction.

On Saturday, the 2nd of September, within a week of the surrender of the town, a portion of the Parliamentarian army received its order to march. The certain success of the anti-Royalists was not yet fully secured. Rumours prevailed of the expected approach of the Prince of Wales with the revolted portion of the fleet at Yarmouth, and the regiments of Colonel Whalley and of Colonel Barkstead were despatched to effect the greater security of this important seaport. The regiment of Colonel Rains-

borough was ordered to Scarborough, the castle of
which town was still held in opposition to the Parliament's forces.

Sir Thomas Fairfax delayed his own departure
until Tuesday, the 5th of September. He devoted the
ensuing fortnight to visiting the towns and garrisons
in the eastern counties. "He was received every-
where as a hero and a conqueror.

> ' The matrons flung their gloves,
> Ladies and maids their scarfs and handkerchiefs,
> Upon him as he passed ; the commons made
> A shower and thunder with their caps and shouts.'

On his approaching the town of Ipswich the mayor,
aldermen, town councillors, and sheriffs, with sword
and mace, in their red gowns, on horseback, met
his Excellency a mile from the town, and, after the
town clerk had congratulated him with a long speech,
accompanied him into the town, where a regiment
of foot stood as a guard to his quarters, and there
gave him divers volleys. The town not only feasted
his Excellency and the attendants with him, but
sent to all the inns to desire them to take no money
for horse-meat or otherwise of any that had relation
to his Excellency." Norwich and the other towns
did, in the language of the news-books of the day,
equalise this entertainment. At Yarmouth more

special rejoicings took place, "the town and ships discharging above one hundred pieces of ordnance, both at his advent and at his farewell."

While General Fairfax was thus honoured by his countrymen,

> " Courted and caressed,
> High plac'd in hall, a welcome guest,"

a very different treatment awaited those who at the taking of Colchester had surrendered to his mercy. The greater part of these soldiers were exposed to much suffering. The Londoners especially were singled out for severity. They were for the most part sent to Bristol to be transported thence beyond sea, either to Ireland for service of war, or as slaves to America, or to some other colony or plantation. The Kentish men, with the others, were removed to the castles and fortresses most distant from their respective homes, as Oxford, Lynn, Warwick, Pendennis, St. Michael's Mount, Arundel, Gloucester, Hereford, and Cardiff. Until the Parliamentary army was broken up and removed from Colchester these prisoners were confined in the churches of the Hyth, Grinsted, Wyvenhoe, and other neighbouring villages. In their march also to the castles assigned for their confinement they mostly rested for the night in the parish churches on straw littered down on the

L

pavement with scant supply, and were stripped,
robbed, and beaten by their guards, and fed on
coarse and insufficient food. The gentlemen were
committed to the custody of individual officers and
troopers until they could gain their liberty by the
payment of a ransom. On the same day that Fairfax
broke up his camp at head-quarters the Lords Norwich,
Loughborough, and Arthur Capel, were removed to
Windsor Castle by the express order of Parliament.
They passed through London with their guards about
five o'clock in the evening of Thursday, the 7th day
of September. Such was the illustration by actual
experience of the interpretation put by the victors on
the term " surrendered to mercy " : the soldiers not
dismissed on parole to their homes, but carried away
to distant military fortresses, and thence transported
as conscripts to a hated service, or as slaves to
American or other colonial masters ; the officers left
to the tender mercies of their captors for ransom,
or consigned as State prisoners to the keep of
Windsor.

It may be worth while to inquire what share Sir
Thomas Fairfax had in the final scenes of the sad
tragedy recorded in this and in the preceding chapter.
Was he the author or the willing accomplice in its
enactments, or was he only the passive agent and
instrument in carrying out the designs of others ?

Every act related of Fairfax through the whole of
his military career, with this single exception, testifies
to his humanity. He himself, in the preliminary
negotiations to this surrender of the town, could
venture to appeal to his habitual sentiments of
clemency. "Neither" (he says, in discussing with
the Royalist Commissioners the question of " mercy ")
" hath he given cause to doubt of his civility to such
he shall retaine prisoners."   The recognised honesty
of Fairfax forbids the supposition that these expressions were used as a blind to deceive the Royalists,
but tends rather to the conclusion that his own
intentions were to treat them with leniency, and
without effusion of blood.   The hesitation and vacil-
lation shown by Sir Thomas Fairfax in the debate
in the council chamber of the Moot Hall on the
morrow of the surrender are inconsistent with the
belief in any predetermined strong purpose on his
part of summary vengeance and punishment. It is
further remarkable that his every allusion to the
execution of the two chief Royalist commanders par-
takes in a greater or less degree of an apologetical
character.   In his first communication to the Earl of
Manchester as the Speaker of the House of Peers, he
defends his conduct with much circumlocution, " as
affording some satisfaction to military justice, and in
part of avenge for the innocent blood they (the Royalist

leaders) had caused to be spilt, and the trouble,
damage, and mischiefe they had brought upon the
towns, the country, and the kingdom." He then expresses a hope (thereby inferring a doubt) that the proceeding would meet the approval of Parliament. In the
later portion of his days, some twenty years after the
event itself, when writing the memorials of his life in
cool moments of reflection, amongst the shades and
retirement of Nun-Monkton, his country seat in York-
shire, he again refers to the subject, and offers an
extenuation of his conduct, by speaking of Sir Charles
Lucas and Sir George Lisle as " soldiers of fortune,
falling into his hands by chance of war." None,
however, knew better than Fairfax himself the fallacy
of this pleading. His opponents in the siege of
Colchester—the great episode of his life—were not
more entitled to be called adventurers than himself.
They were free-born Englishmen, of good estate,
ancient lineage, long settled in the land, honoured
with the commissions of their sovereign, and engaged
in a noble contest for the ancient laws, customs, and
constitution of the realm.   These lame excuses served
better than none as salves of his conscience and pal-
liations of his conduct.   The real truth, the certain
key-note to his proceedings, is revealed in these same
" Memorials."   He has left an authoritative record
under his own hand of the position he held in regard

to his council of war. " My commission as Generall"
(he says) "obliged me to act with Councel ; but the
arbitrary and unlimited power of this Councel would
act without a General, and all I could do was ineffectual to oppose them." And in another passage
he states his position with regard to his council of
war yet more plainly : "I say from the time they
declared their usurped authority at Triplow Heath
(May, 1646) I never gave my free consent to anything
they did ; but being yet undischarged of my place,
they set my name in a way of course to all their
papers, whether I consented or not."*

This recalcitrant and tyrannical council of war,
which Fairfax was powerless to resist, was animated
at this time by peculiarly exasperated feelings against
Charles I. and his supporters. It was mainly composed of those very men who had at an early period
of this year conceived the design of bringing their
sovereign to a public trial, and had prepared the way
by refusing to hold any communication with him.
The Royalists, by their simultaneous risings and
spirited efforts, had compelled the renewal of proposals
for a treaty. The purpose of Ireton, Fleetwood, and
of other chief leaders in Fairfax's Council, was to put
a stop to this treaty, to break off all communications

* "Short Memorials of Thomas, Lord Fairfax," written by himself,
pp. 104, 124, 126. London, 1699.

with the King, to resume the position they had assumed before the present war arose, and to persevere in their purpose of bringing the King to a public trial and ignominious death. Colonel Ludlow states in his Memoirs, "that he visited Fairfax in his camp at Colchester to try and induce him to join in putting an end to the treaty then in progress, but that he found him indisposed to assist his plans."* The leaders of his council-at-war were less scrupulous, and entered heartily into the scheme proposed. There is, therefore, abundant reason to suppose that the evil treatment of the soldiers who surrendered at Colchester, the violent and hasty deaths of Sir Charles Lucas and Sir George Lisle, the detention of Lords Norwich, Loughborough, and Capel, as State prisoners in the power of the Parliament, were parts of a fixed plan, which was designed to culminate in a deeper crime and darker vengeance meditated towards the sovereign, a captive himself in the hands of the Parliament. The true solution, therefore, of Fairfax's conduct is this: His own personal feelings inclined him to a course of mercy, but he was overruled by his council of war, who would have no denial nor contradiction of their plans. He was of too humane a disposition to institute any new, unprecedented method of exacting retribution, or to sacrifice human life in a spirit of

* "Memoirs of Edward Ludlow, Esq.," vol. I., p. 262.

retaliation or revenge.   But through the infirmity of his weakness and irresolution he became the instrument in the hand of others, and allowed actions to be done under the shelter of his honourable name which he never sanctioned, and of which in his inner conscience he never approved.   Such must ever be the penalty of good men who have not the courage of their own convictions, but become the tools of others bolder and more unscrupulous than themselves.

CHAPTER XI.

THE FINAL RETRIBUTION.

> . . . . . . " Be just, and fear not.
> Let all the ends thou aim'st at be
> Thy God's and Truth's : then, when thou fall'st,
> Thou fall'st a blessed martyr."
>
> SHAKESPEARE.

The final fortunes of Lord Loughborough—The narrow escape of Lord
  Norwich — Biography of Arthur Lord Capel — His escape from
  the Tower, and re-capture—His verses in the Tower—His medita-
  tions—An account of his trial—His three appearances before the
  Court—His demeanour therein—An affecting scene in the House of
  Commons—Arthur Lord Capel's last letter to his wife—Doctor
  George Morley—His account of Arthur Lord Capel's last hours—
  His final interview with his wife, and his last advice to his son—
  His conduct upon the scaffold—Its construction and accessories—
  Behaviour of Lord Capel—His address to the bystanders, and to the
  executioner—His last prayers—The results of his execution—Con-
  clusion.

No record of the famous siege of Colchester can be
complete which fails to give an account of the fate,
fortunes, and final retribution of the three chief actors
in its exciting incidents, Lord Norwich, Lord Loughborough, and Arthur Lord Capel.

The story of Lord Loughborough is soon told.
After a six months' imprisonment, partly in Windsor
Castle and partly in the Tower of London, he

compounded with the Parliament by the payment of a large fine in money, and was allowed to retire and live on his own estate without fear of molestation.

Lord Norwich experienced a much narrower escape. Arraigned before that relentless tribunal which had just condemned his sovereign, he was sentenced by the majority of the court to suffer the extreme penalty of the scaffold. He appealed, however, to the Parliament itself, and, "being a man of jovial and hearty temperament, with few, if any, personal enemies, and, above all, having shown much reverence and submission before his judges," he obtained at the last moment a reprieve from the very gates of death by the single casting vote of Sir William Lenthall, the Speaker of the House of Commons.

The fortunes of the third sufferer in this list of worthies will require a longer history. Arthur Capel, knight of the shire for Herts in the Parliaments of 1639 and 1641, created, A.D. 1641, Baron Capel by Charles I., was the owner of Hadham and of other extensive estates in the county of Hertford. At the commencement of the civil war he formed his dependants into a troop, and joined the Royal army, and was appointed Lieutenant-General, under Prince Rupert, of the counties of Worcester, Salop, Chester, and the six northern counties of Wales. In his military command he proved himself a strict disci-

plinarian, and especially endeavoured to prevent his
troops from any spoil, robbery, oppression, plunder,
or pillage of the King's subjects.*   Endowed with a
fine intellect, polished manners, manly grace of form,
and excellent judgment, he was chosen by the King
to be the tutor and governor of his eldest son, the
Prince of Wales.   He consequently left England
with his royal charge, the heir apparent, after the
surrender of the city of Exeter to the Parliament,
A.D. 1644, and resided for two or three years in Paris.
At the conclusion of the first civil war, A.D. 1646,
he returned to England, and lived in quiet retirement
on his own estate, until in A.D. 1648, alarmed at the
threatened destruction of his sovereign by the Parliament, he took up arms in his defence, and became by
his personal courage, noble example, and admirable
aptitude for command (as has been shown in the
preceding chapters), the most influential leader of
the Royalists in their deeds of daring, and the most
energetic encourager of their efforts for the deliverance
of their sovereign.   The short span of life allowed to
Lord Capel after the termination of the siege of
Colchester was full of remarkable incident and
adventure.   Confined in the first instance for three
long months in Windsor Castle, he was transferred
in the middle of December to the more gloomy

* See his address to his soldiers, B. M. Collection, $\frac{869}{1}$, F. 7.

custody of the Tower of London, as the fortress at Windsor was allotted to the exclusive occupation of the King, received on the evening of Saturday, the 23rd of December, as a State prisoner within its walls. Fully convinced of the power and malice of his enemies, and of the determination of the Parliament to take his life, he saw no hope of safety but in an escape from his imprisonment; and this he successfully accomplished on the evening of Saturday, January 27th, 1648-9,* two days before the execution of his beloved sovereign, Charles I. Provided with a long cord by the kindness of his friends, he let himself down from the window of his chamber, and in spite of the difficulty experienced in crossing the moat, in which, though a tall and athletic man, he left his cloak behind him, he reached in safety the friends who were waiting for him, and obtained by their aid a refuge on the night of his flight at chambers in the Temple. Afraid to remain there, he took a boat at the Temple Stairs in the dusk of the next evening, and directed the wherryman to make for a house in Lambeth; but, from some faultiness in his disguise, or from his own striking figure, or, as is commonly asserted, by the inadvertent use of his title by his companion, the waterman

* The year was counted to and from March 25th, not as now from January 1st.

whom he employed discovered him, and for the sake of the reward of £40 offered for his re-capture, instantly on leaving the boat went to the captain of the guard in charge of the House of Commons, and offered himself as the guide to a company of soldiers, who effectually secured his person.

Thus, within the space of thirty hours, replaced in the prison from which he had escaped, watched with a greater severity of strictness, overwhelmed with a sense of the cruel martyrdom of his beloved sovereign, and convinced of the nearness of his own approaching fate, Lord Capel devoted the solitary hours of his second imprisonment in the Tower to deep thought and serious meditation. The following stanzas form a portion of a poem composed by him after his second consignment to this ancient fortress. They not only possess merit as verses, but are more valuable as bearing testimony to the ease of mind and to the cheerful and patient resignation with which he endured his grievous flight of afflictions.

STANZAS WRITTEN BY LORD CAPEL, WHEN A
PRISONER IN THE TOWER.

1.

" That which the world miscalls a jayl,
  A private closet is to me ;
Whilst a good conscience is my bail,
  And innocence my liberty.
Locks, bars, and solitude together met,
Make me no prisoner, but an anchoret.

2.

" The cynich hugs his poverty,
  The pelican her wilderness ;
And 'tis the Indian's pride to be
  Naked on frozen Caucasus.
Contentment feels no smart ; Stoics we see
Make torments easy by their apathy.

3. .

" My soul is free as is th' ambient air,
  Which doth my outward parts include
Whilst loyal thoughts do still repair,
  To company my solitude.
What tho' they do with chains my body bind,
My King can only captivate my mind."*

These two meditations were also written in the
Tower :—

" God's secret will is unknown. Whatever it be, His name be magnified. My duty is to walk by the revealed and acknowledged rules of
His truth, and the received precepts of virtue, which through my
frailty I have not practised so well as I should, and as I wish I had ;
yet never shall the fear of death (by His divine and gracious assistance), no, not in the ugliest shape attired, daunt me from asserting
them."

" I know my cause is good, and that my sufferings answer not the
value and worthiness of it. I know that my Redeemer liveth, that
died for me. Most willingly I die for His truth, and for acting my
duty to His servant the King, whom He hath placed here upon his
terrestrial throne amongst us. I know and believe that to die is gain,
the gaining of an immortal and incorruptible life, with eternal felicity
in the sight of God our Saviour, and His blessed angels.

              " My Saviour the Cross sanctifi'd ;
                My King the block hath dignifi'd.
                Crosses nor blocks I do not fear ;
                Sanctifi'd, dignifi'd, they are.
                        Gloria Deo in excelsis."

* *Gentleman's Magazine,* 1751, p. 82.

The sad presentiments of Lord Capel were to be speedily fulfilled. On Monday, February the 5th, precisely seven days after the death of the King, the court which had passed on him the sentence of condemnation was formally re-constituted by the sanction of Parliament for the trial and for the foredetermined and premeditated destruction of the five chief Loyalist leaders—the Duke of Hamilton, the General of the Scottish army; the Earl of Holland, who had headed a rising of the county of Bedford; the Earl of Norwich and Lord Capel, the main defenders of Colchester against the Parliament; and Sir John Owen, implicated in the loyal insurrections in Wales. This devotion to the late King was their chief fault before the judges who had sanctioned his execution. The emergencies of the times, and the fears of a popular reaction on the part of the members of the court, forbade any lengthened or ceremonious proceedings. Quick despatch was the order of the day. The whole trial, though involving the lives of five eminent citizens, did not occupy a month.

The court met for the first time for actual business on Saturday, February 10th, with a considerable outward observance of pomp and solemnity. The president, Bradshaw, occupied a canopied chair, robed in his scarlet gown and massive S.S. chain. The

golden mace of the Speaker of the House of Commons
was placed on the table before him. The avenues
and entrances of the court were filled with soldiers.

Lord Capel, on being placed at the bar, treated the
president and judges with the utmost contempt, made
not the slightest gesture of greeting or obeisance, but
looked round on the spectators with a stern air of
severe displeasure. Being called on by the court to
plead to the indictment read against him, he referred
to the articles of the surrender of Colchester, declared
that the word of the General, Sir Thomas Fairfax,
had been given for his life, and asserted with an
authoritative voice that "not all the magistrates in
Christendom could rightfully call him to further
question."

Lord Capel was brought for a second time to the bar
of the court on Tuesday, the 13th of February, when
Fairfax himself was summoned to give his version of
the statements made by him at his first examination.
Sir Thomas Fairfax, more anxious for his own
reputation with his party than for the safety of his
late persevering antagonist, declared to the court
with characteristic caution that what he had promised
on the surrender of Colchester was "a freedom from
execution of the sword, and not an exemption from
the proceedings of a civil court at the pleasure of
Parliament."

Lord Capel received one more summons to appear before the court on Wednesday, the 21st of February, and on his third and last appearance he pleaded his own cause with much pathos and eloquence in a speech of some hours, in which he vindicated his conduct by references to Magna Charta, the laws of the land, the privilege of peerage, the *jus gentium*, and the particular promises of Fairfax on his surrender.

His pleas and arguments were overruled by the law officers of the court, and by the authority of its president. After the delay of a few days, during which the trials of his fellow-prisoners were brought to a close, he was brought before the court on the morning of Tuesday, March 6th, to hear the sentence of his condemnation, and to be given over formally to the civil authorities, the sheriffs of Middlesex, as a traitor to the State.

The English House of Commons has witnessed through the lengthened period of its eventful history many a scene of deep and intensely thrilling interest. None, however, in all the records of its annals can exceed, if indeed any can equal, that which was exhibited within its walls on the day succeeding the condemnation of Lord Capel and of his companions in misfortune.

A large group of ladies, the noblest and stateliest

in the land, arrayed in the deepest mourning, preceded by a mace-bearer of the House, and accompanied by men of the highest position in the country,
walked up to the table of the House, and, with pale
faces, hysterical sobs, copious tears, and all the
telling tokens of womanly sorrow, presented on
bended knees a petition to the Speaker for the lives
of their husbands or fathers under the sentence of a
fatal condemnation.   In the midst of this fair bevy
of noble dames were the proud Countess of Manchester, the wife of the Speaker of the very recently
abolished House of Lords ; the wealthy and aged
Lady Holland ; the virtuous and highly gifted Lady
Arthur Capel ; the youthful Lady Rich, and divers
other ladies of rank, title, and influence.   Among
the men were the Earl of Warwick, then Lord High
Admiral of England, a brother of one of the
condemned lords ; the Lord Rich, who had fought
for the Parliament ; Lords Beauchamp and Newport;
the youthful son of Lord Capel (who had been a
hostage in Fairfax's camp, and was just of age), and
other gentlemen of high reputation.   Never did a more
moving spectacle appeal to the sympathies of fellow-
citizens and fellow-countrymen.   But the effort was
in vain.   Neither the tears of those noble ladies, nor
the services of those noble men, were effectual to
move the relentless fanaticism which ruled supreme

M

in that assembly. A long debate ensued, but a large majority confirmed the fatal verdict on the three most illustrious prisoners.* On the names of each being singly in succession submitted to the House, the Duke of Hamilton, the Earl of Holland, and Lord Capel were left without reprieve to the judgment of the court. Sir John Owen escaped by the narrow margin of three or four voices, while Lord Norwich, as has been already stated, was only saved by the casting vote of Lenthall.

Lord Capel was fully prepared for this final confirmation of the adverse sentence recorded against him. He set himself at once to meet with manly resolution his inevitable fate. He wrote this affecting letter, the very model of affectionate Christian valediction, to his wife, on the night preceding his execution :—

" MY DEAREST LIFE,

" My eternal life is in Christ Jesus. My worldly consideration in the highest degree thou hast deserved. Let me live long in thy dear memory, to

* No prouder eulogium ever immortalised the name and character of a man than that pronounced by Cromwell, when voting upon the petition for the life of Lord Capel. " Cromwell, who had known him very well, spake so much good of him, and professed to have so much kindness and respect for him, that all men thought he was now safe ; when he concluded, that his affection to the public so. much weighed down his private friendship that he could not but tell them, that the question was now whether they would preserve the most bitter and implacable enemy they now had ; that he knew the Lord Capel very well, and

the comfort of my family, our dear children, whom God out of mercy in Christ hath bestowed on us. I beseech thee, take care of thy health. Sorrow not unsoberly, unusually. God be unto thee better than an husband, and to my children better than a father. I am sure He is able to be so. God be with thee, my most virtuous wife. God multiply many comforts to thee and my dear children, is the fervent prayer of thy dearest husband,

"ARTHUR CAPEL."

The presence of a wise and affectionate counsellor is the source of unspeakable comfort on the bed of sickness or in the expectation of death. Lord Capel amidst all his troubles did not lack at this trying crisis a friend and adviser well qualified to assist him by his counsels and prayers in his painful approaching exodus. Doctor George Morley, who after the Restoration became the celebrated Bishop of Winchester, acted as his chaplain, and has written a most interesting record of his last few hours upon earth. The account is most touching in its simple pathos,

---

knew that he would be the last man in England that would forsake the Royal interest; that he had great courage, industry, and generosity; that he had many friends who would always adhere to him ; and that as long as he lived, what condition soever he was in, he would be a thorn in their sides ; and therefore, for the good of the Commonwealth, he should give his vote against the petition."—Lord Clarendon, "History of the Great Rebellion," book xi., § 260. Oxford, 1869.

and exhibits just such a portraiture as might have
been looked for in so good a father, so loyal a patriot,
so high principled a man, and so true a Christian as
Arthur Lord Capel.

"I was there at the time assigned, viz., the
morning on which he was to suffer, and after some
short conference he desired me to hear him pray,
which he did for half-an-hour in an excellent method,
very apt expressions, and most strong, hearty, and
passionate affections—*first* confessing and bewailing
his sins with strong cries and tears, then humbly and
most earnestly desiring God's mercies through the
merits of Christ only; *secondly*, for his dear wife and
children, with some passion, but for her specially with
most ardent affections, recommending them to the
Divine Providence with great confidence and assurance, and desiring for them rather the blessing of a
better life than of this; *thirdly*, for the King, Church,
and State; and *lastly*, for his enemies, with almost
the same ardour and affection.

"After this, sending for my Lord of Norwich and
Sir John Owen, I read the whole office of the Church
for Good Friday; and then, after a short homily, we
received the Sacrament, in which action he behaved
himself with great humility, zeal, and devotion. And
being demanded after we had done how he found
himself, he replied, very much *better, stronger, cheer-*

fuller for that *heavenly repast,* and that he doubted not to walk like a Christian through the vale of death in the strength of it. But he was to have an *Agony* before his *Passion;* and that was the parting with his wife and eldest son . . . which, indeed, was the saddest spectacle that ever I beheld. In which occasion he could not choose but confess a little of human frailty; yet even then he did not forget both to comfort and counsel her, and the rest of his friends; particularly in blessing the young lord, he commanded him never to revenge his death, though it should be in his power. The like he said unto his lady. He told his son he would leave him a legacy out of David's Psalms, and that was this, Lord, lead me in a plain way: ' For, boy,' said he, ' I would have you a plain, honest man, and hate dissimulation.'

" After this, with much ado, I persuaded his wife and the rest to be gone; and then, being all alone with me, he said, ' Doctor, the hardest part of my work in this world is now past; ' meaning the parting with his wife. Then he desired me to pray prepara- tively to his death, that in the last action he might so behave himself as might be most for God's glory, for the endearing his dead master's memory, his pre- sent master's service, and that he might avoid the doing or saying of anything which might savour either of vanity or sullenness.

" This being done, he was, with the other lords, carried privately in a sedan chair to Sir Thomas Cotton's house (close beside Westminster Hall), where I was with him till he was called unto the scaffold, and would have gone up with him, but the guard of soldiers would not suffer me."

The conduct of Lord Capel upon the scaffold was consistent with these exalted supplications. With him there was no dissimulation, no display of hollow bravery, nor pretence of Roman resolution. Everything he said and did was with a purpose. Under the constraint of a deep responsibility, under the sense of a pure motive, strengthened by dependence upon Divine aid, he sought, both by speech and action, to do honour to his late royal master, to glorify his God, and, whilst he forgave the personal injury to himself, to protest against the usurped authority of those who caused his death.

The immediate incidents of his execution deserve a particular narration. At ten o'clock in the morning of Friday, the 9th day of March, he was conveyed from the Tower privately in a sedan chair, guarded by a company of soldiers, to the house of Sir Thomas Cotton,* which closely adjoined Westminster Hall.

* Son of Sir Robert Bruce Cotton, the eminent antiquary, and founder of the Cotton Library, the valuable books of which were transferred to the British Museum in 1753.

Precisely at noon on that same day, the Duke of Hamilton, and, about one hour after him, the Earl of Holland, had suffered—the first with noble heroism, and the latter with an occasional exhibition of the weakness inherent in humanity under such an agony of trial. Lord Capel, as the lowest in rank, was the last to receive the fatal summons; and very remarkable was the scene as he passed to his euthanasia.

The day was unusually fine, inviting to life. A light breeze gently ruffled the then limpid Thames, visible from the place of execution. The sun shone brightly in the heavens, lighting up with its glow the houses, the crowd, the helmets, breastplates, weapons of the soldiers, and all the solemn paraphernalia prepared for the occasion. The scaffold was a huge wooden platform, erected in the Palace Yard, on the north side of Westminster Hall. In the centre lay the fatal block, of massive wood, placed in accordance with the directions of President Bradshaw and his colleagues in such a position that Lord Capel and his fellow-sufferers should be compelled in the very moment of death to look towards the chamber of the court that condemned them, and whose authority they had disputed. By the block stood the executioner, his face concealed by a black mask or vizor, and his hands resting on a large-headed, long-handled axe, which touched the floor. At a little

distance, but within sight, was the velvet-covered
coffin, prepared for the removal of the corpse. The
other persons, either in the routine of duty or by the
permission of privilege, occupying the scaffold were the
Sheriffs of Middlesex and of the City of London, in
their robes of office ; two clerks—in modern language,
shorthand writers or reporters—seated at small desks
or tables, to take down what was spoken ; the officer
in command of the guard for the day, Lieutenant-
Colonel Becher, with some few of his men armed
with halberds ; and the domestic servants attached
to the household of Lord Capel. Below, in immediate contiguity with the scaffold, were companies
of foot-guards from the regiments of Colonels Pride
and Hewson, and squadrons of horse from Fairfax's
own regiment. These in serried ranks surrounded
three sides of the scaffold, and behind them was a
great concourse of people. The face of the scaffold,
fronting Charing Cross, was protected by a low rail,
at which the noble sufferers stood to address the
populace. The entrance to the scaffold was the large
northern gates of Westminster Hall, which were
thrown wide open. A passage from these gates, up
the centre of the Hall, to the apartments of Sir
Thomas Cotton's house, was kept clear by a rank of
halberdiers on either side, behind whom stood a
crowd of the more privileged spectators.

Between these lines of living men, came Lord
Capel, about two o'clock on that bright, pleasant day,
preceded by the sheriffs, surrounded by a small body-
guard of soldiers, and closely accompanied by his
chaplain, Doctor Morley. He was dressed in a sad-
coloured suit, and short cloak, and shoes and stockings.
He had his hat cocked on his head, and carried a cloak
under his arm. On the passage from the house to
the scaffold he put off his hat to the people on both
sides, and looked austerely about him. The end of
the Hall being reached, permission to ascend the
scaffold was denied to Dr. Morley, as being an Epis-
copalian. Lord Capel took a manly and hurried
leave of him, and ascended the steps with his hat on.
He regarded the soldiers and populace " without sign
of fear, or any show of death approaching,"* and
" trod the fatal stage with all the dignity of valour
and conscious integrity." After a few moments he
made inquiry of Colonel Becher whether the Lords
had spoken with their hats off. Receiving an answer
in the affirmative, he came to the front of the scaffold,
and, having taken off his hat, addressed the people
" with much earnestness, as if a minister had been in
a pulpit, rather than like a man dying."† He declared his forgiveness of his judges ; his firm adher-

* News-Books of the Day. E. King's Pamphlets. Brit. Mus. 527.
† Walpole's Works, vol. I., p. 360.

ence to the Christian faith, as taught in the Church of
England ; his conviction that no law of this or of any
other country sanctioned his execution, after admission to quarter ; his comfort in believing that he died
for obedience to the law of God, especially mentioning the fifth commandment as the foundation of all
government and magistracy. He then expressed his
personal sorrow at having voted for the condemnation
of Earl Strafford, " out of cowardice and not out of
malice ; " his perfect willingness to suffer for his dear
master the late king; his prayers for the greater
happiness of the present king, his late master's son ;
and, finally, reiterated his assurance of Divine mercy,
and his prayers for blessings upon his country, and
upon all the people in the land. After he had concluded his speech, he spoke a word to his servant
Baldwin, and sent a loving message to his wife ; and
then calling to him the executioner, he gave him five
pounds, with a request that his body might only be
touched by his own servants, and said to him, "Honest
man, I have forgiven thee, and therefore strike boldly
—from my soul I do it." After this he once again
went to the front of the scaffold, and said to the
people : " Gentlemen, though I doubt it not of you,
yet I think it convenient to ask it of you, that you
would join in prayers with me that God would merci-
fully receive my soul, and that for His alone mercies

in Christ Jesus. God Almighty keep you all." Then, kneeling before the block, he lifted up his hands and eyes towards heaven, and then lay down. A little incident occurred here, as will often happen in the most solemn scenes, which somewhat discomposed him. The collar of his shirt was found to be too high—"for though he was tall, yet had he but a short neck"—so that he rose up again, and had some help. He then, as he stood, lifted up his hands and eyes, and said in a low but distinct voice, " O God, I do with a perfect and willing heart submit to Thy will. O God, I do most willingly humble myself." Then kneeling down again, he placed his neck on the block, and having stretched both his hands forward beyond his head, said to the executioner, "When I lift up my hand, then you may strike." In a brief space, after a short private prayer, amidst a most intense silence, he lifted up his right hand, and at one blow his head was severed from the body. His servants reverently placed his honoured remains* in the coffin, and bore them from the scaffold.

* Arthur Lord Capel was buried at Little Hadham on the 20th day of March. This inscription was placed on his tomb after the Restoration :—

"Here lyeth interred the body of Arthur, Lord Capel, Baron of Hadham, who was murdered for his loyalty to King Charles the First. March 9, 1648."

Lord Capel married Elizabeth, daughter and sole heiress of Sir Charles Morrison, Bart., K.B., of Cassiobury, Herts. He left four sons and four daughters. His four sons were, 1. Arthur, his heir, created Viscount

So died the good, gallant, but unfortunate Arthur Capel. His glory was, that having shunned the splendours of his master's throne, he stood forward as its most prominent defender in its fall. His spotless life, unselfish gallantry, and unmerited execution gave such a moral dignity to the cause he espoused, that he is declared " like Samson, to have done his foes more harm at his death than in all his life, by raising and renewing the desires of the people "* for a restoration of the monarchy. These lines, written in honour of one higher in rank than himself, and, at least in his last moments, equally heroic, may well describe his bearing at the scene of his execution :—

> " While round the armed bands
> Did clasp their bloody hands,
> He nothing common did or mean,
> Amid that memorable scene ;
> But with his keener eye
> The axe's edge did try.†

Maldon and Earl of Essex, 20th of April, 1661 ; 2. Henry, created a Knight of the Bath at the Restoration, and after serving in the House of Commons, advanced to the peerage as Baron Capel of Tewkesbury, April 11, 1692 ; he was made Lord-lieutenant of Ireland, and died in Dublin Castle May 30, 1696 ; 3. Edward ; 4. Charles. None of these three sons had any children. His daughters were, 1. Mary, wife 1st of Henry Seymour, Lord Beauchamp, and 2ndly of Henry Somerset, Duke of Beaufort ; 2. Elizabeth, wife of Charles Dormer, Earl of Carnarvon ; 3. Theodosia, wife of Henry Hyde, Earl of Clarendon ; 4. Anne, wife of Giles Strangwayes, Esquire, of Melbury Sampford, Dorset.

* Heath's " Chronicon," p. 424.

† Charles I. cautioned a gentleman on the scaffold not to approach too near the axe, lest he should touch its edge.

" Nor called the gods, with vulgar spite,
  To vindicate his helpless right ;
    But bowed his comely head
    Down as upon a bed."*

Such is the final record of events intimately connected with the famous siege of Colchester, the chief
actors in which—the heroes of this history—were remarkable for the singleness of their minds, the purity
of their motives, and the valiancy of their actions,
no less than for the charitable forgiveness of their
enemies, the marvellous fortitude and noble dignity
of their deaths, and for their heroic submission to an
unduly severe

FINAL RETRIBUTION.

* Andrew Marvell.

CHAPTER XII.

SOME OF LORD CAPEL'S "DAILY OBSERVATIONS, OR MEDITATIONS DIVINE AND MORAL."

"Proverbs certainly are of excellent use ; they are mucrones verborum, pointed speeches, they serve to be interlaced in continual speech, they serve upon particular occasions, if you take out the kernel of them, and make them your own."—LORD BACON.

LORD CAPEL may rightly be considered, as the hero of the siege of Colchester. He has left a small volume of "Daily Observations or Meditations," which illustrate his character and help to show the principles by which he was actuated. Less proverbial than the "Adagia" of Erasmus, less anecdotal than the apothegms of Lord Bacon, less cynical than the "Lacon" of Colton, yet more varied in their experience of men and manners than the "Table Talk" of Martin Luther or of Coleridge, and more solid in their reasonings than the utterances of "Helps' Friends in Council," these short contemplations will be found true to the universal nature and constitution of man. Free from all savour of religious bigotry, and from the jargon of any peculiar political opinions, lofty in principle, excellent in matter, wise in council, and sound in judgment, they will recommend themselves alike to the young and old as "pointed speeches," as fit samples of holy thought and godly resolutions.

"DAILY OBSERVATIONS, OR MEDITATIONS DIVINE AND MORAL," BY LORD ARTHUR CAPEL.

I.

If a man in innocency needed a help, solace, and comfort, and marriage was all these, how deficient were our (now miserable) lives without it. For besides that it doubles joys and divides griefs, it creates new and unthought-of contentment; and yet I have observed many that lose the blessings of wedlock, nay worse, that of good wine have made the sharpest vinegar.

II.

Recreations have their due place in our life, and not without good profit both to the mind and body;

to the *body* for *health*, to the *mind* for *refreshing*
Yet we may observe many that perpetually live in
them, not *using* but *serving* them, and so over-
mastered by them that their best fortunes are not
employed so willingly to the advantage of any
necessary or good occasion as to be engulphed in
idle pastime.   This is too frequent a vanity.

III.

In economical government, as it is discretion in
the master of a family not to neglect severe discipline
towards the insolent and wilful faults of his servants,
so it is not less wisdom favourably to receive an
ingenuous acknowledgment from them of those slips
which human frailty or inevitable chance may cast
upon them.   For their hire commands but the *hands'*
service, but 'tis gentle goodness invites the *heart's*
affection ; and a wise man would willingly have his
servants (as I may call them) his *servile friends*.

IV.

Few there are but do love knowledge ; but the
reason why there are so few that are knowing is
because *the entrance of all arts and sciences is*
difficult ; and though most are delighted with the
amiable parts of *learning* or *wisdom* in other men,
and desire to be like qualified, yet they imitate not

their indefatigable *industry* by which they ascended
to that eminent *height*.

V.

If God should have demanded of man *how many
days of seven he would give to His service*, three,
I am persuaded, would have been the fewest as
being but the lesser part of seven. And what
good nature can willingly deny *half* to Him that
gave *all?* But God dealing so graciously as to
separate but *one*, how greatly should His goodness
incite us not to deprive Him of the least minute of
it, nay, not to cast a thought towards our worldly
business or pleasures on that day.

VI.

I observe divers who have many affairs that by
the infelicity of *one* are so distempered that they
lose all consideration to guide themselves in the rest.
Nay, *the loss of a trifle shall nullify all the content-
ments of millions of enjoyed blessings*, like that
master of a ship that should neglect the *compass,
mainmast*, and *stern* of the ship because some slight
flag is lost.

VII.

*Biting jests, the more truth they carry with them,
the broader-scarred memory they leave behind them.*

N

Many times they are like the wounds of *chewed bullets*, where the *ruggedness* causeth almost incurable hurts.

VIII.

Unhappy they are who never know their friends but when they are gone : first, in losing the comfort of them when they may have it ; next, in desiring and wanting them, when they are past hope of having them.

IX.

Nemo nascitur sapiens, nay, a man cannot be virtuous without adversity. Where were patience without crosses ? where fortitude without resistance ? and so all the rest have their opposites for exercise. Never was excellent piece of work made without cuttings, nor wise man without afflictions. Therefore it were *folly to fear them;* and (no paradox to say) *unhappy to want them :* but *wisdom it is to profit by them.*

X.

In this tempestuous world no line holds anchor so fast as a good conscience. Man's favour is but a fine thread, that will scarcely hold one tug of a crafty tale-bearer. But this is a cable so strong, that when force is offered to it, the straining rather strengthens, by uniting the parts more close.

XI.

Unhappy is the man that steers the comfort of his life by the pleasing of others. But let us make honesty the mark we sail by, and so steadily let it be, that we neither advance forwarder for vain applause, nor retire for fear of detraction.

XII.

The wearied man desires the bed, the discontented man the grave. Both would fain be at rest.

XIII.

Two sorts of enemies most dangerous, and both inseparable from the miserable condition of most of all men; but altogether of men of great fortunes; the *flatterer*, the *lyar*. One strikes *before*, the other *behind;* both *insensibly*, both *dangerously*.

XIV.

In *heat of argument* men are commonly like those that are tyed *back to back*, close joined, and yet they cannot *see one another*.

XV.

Among all the conditions that men are sorted into there is none that renders perfectly happy. Crowns are set with thorns; with riches desires in-

crease. Honour is envied, often blasted. Poverty
perisheth, and in my estimation the meaner-esteemed
fortunes are really to be valued the better, but especially those that least incite inordinate affections.

XVI.

Expense is not the only thing that cracks men's
estates, but the regardlessness of what and how we
spend. For men of great fortunes I have seen enjoy
no more, neither in substance nor show, than those
of less, who have sided with them in the same courses,
yet the greater have perished, and the less held up.
For the *most provident* may *spend most*.

XVII.

Few have the wisdom in adverse things to use
prevoyrance before them, circumspection in them,
and patience after them ; but are commonly impro-
vident, negligent, and perturbated in the undue season. But in *remediless* occurrences it is the best
wisdom of man to be *insensible*.

XVIII.

To those who are wilfully bent against any good
conceit of us, it will prove but *trouble* without *success*
to endeavour by servile obsequiousness to gain them.
The better way is, by a constant fair carriage, to

expect that time may ripen the fruit which haste cannot ; and too hasty shaking throws down the sour with the sweet.

XIX.

Compliments may be used, but not usually.   They are like sweetmeats* (entertainment for strangers or great personages) which keep their taste, if rarely served, but if commonly, prove nauseous.

XX.

Those whose desires and expectations are mode-rate have their afflictions and troubles not intolerable.

XXI.

Sharp and bitter jests are blunted more by neg-lecting than responding, except they be *suddenly* and *wittingly* retorted.   But it is no imputation of a man's wisdom to use a silent scorn.

XXII.

It requires a good temper to endure contradicting spirits, but they are best silenced by silence.

XXIII.

It is more ingenuous by gentle acknowledgement

* This alludes to a custom of the day, by which the municipal authorities offered "sack and sweetmeats" to illustrious strangers, visiting their towns.

to confess a fault, than with unblushing impudence
to maintain it; and inhumane it is with a proud
arrogance to insult over a penitent delinquent.

XXIV.

No decent fashion is unlawful; and if fashion
be but a diversified decency, without question it is but
a cynical singularity either to exclaim against, or not
sociably to use them.

XXV.

Wealth without *friends* is like *life* without HEALTH.
The one an *uncomfortable fortune*, the other a *miserable being*.

XXVI.

It is a hard thing to be a true friend.   For many
times in acting the part of a true friend to one we love,
we not only lose familiarity, but procure hatred, and
I scarcely know a man that is capable of a true friend.

XXVII.

Our life is but a moment of time between two
eternities of infinite beginning and never ending. It is
the very middle point of a perpendicular line, and but a
punctum, a thing of no sensible being, but imaginary,
from which if we ascend by holy meditations, faith,
and good works, we shall attain to a never-ending
beatitude ; but if from it we descend by carnal

thoughts, sensual appetites, and evil actions, we shall
be perpetuated in everlasting torments.   Great therefore is the consequence of this minute's disposure.
God, I beseech Him, even for my Christ His sake,
often incite me in this meditation.

XXVIII.

In the heat of *summer* we easily believe there
will come a season of *frost* and *snow ;* yet in our
prosperity we consider not of *adversity :* yet the *one*
is as successive as the *other.*

XXIX.

The *idle man* is more perplexed *what to do* than
the *laborious* in doing *what he ought.*

XXX.

Most men that affect sports account them a prin-
cipal part of their life ; and that, I conceive to be
the reason, why they prosecute them with so much
affection, and if crost in them, demonstrate so much
passion.   But to consider truly of them, they are but
pastimes, little removed from lost time ; and if their
insinuating delight do steal us from our more necessary occasions, yet it is absurd to suffer any per-
plexity for them, when they fall out crossly.

XXXI.

Great respect it is to inform a friend wisely

and fully of his error ; but if one perceive him im-
moveable, then it 's better to content ourselves with
the *integrity of our intention* and *faithful respect*
than to proceed further.   For it will be *without profit*
to *both,* it may be with *inconvenience* to *our friend.*
For *the smith's anvil is the harder for blows.*

XXXII.

I will sometimes *conceal a secret* from my most
entire friend, or at least for *some space.*   For otherwise he may think I have delivered the rest more out
of facility than confidence in him ; nay, I will do it
to make trial of myself.

XXXIII.

I never saw men *too anxious* in business, *happy.*
For if they proceed *luckily,* it *prides* them, and they
are *envied ;* if *unfortunately,* it *dejects* them, and
then they are *scorned.*

XXXIV.

If I intend to *give,* I will not so long *delay* as
to suffer *importunity,* for then I rather *sell* than *give ;*
for what is got by prayers, entreaties, submission, is
ever accompanied with shame, and it is a dear purchase that is so bought.   Yet many there are that
never give without it, and have neither the skill nor

generousness to find out fitting objects for their liberality.

XXXV.

A wise man will not speak the truth at all times; nor an honest speak an untruth at any time.

XXXVI.

Quarrels are easily begun, hardly avoided, and difficultly ended. For what one hath done, neither cannot undo; but mutual consent must make the accord perfect.

XXXVII.

In sickness our distemper makes us loath the most natural meat. In anger our fury makes us vilify the most wholesome advices.

XXXVIII.

Obstinacy is advantage to our enemies, trouble to our friends, and the assured overthrow of ourselves.

XXXIX.

It is frequent with many, upon every slight and trivial demand, to pawn *their honour*. A most inconsiderate thing. For what is so often lent, and passeth so many hands upon every occasion, cannot but lose much of its lustre, and receive soile.

XL.

Difficulty of achievement stupifies the sluggard, advises the prudent, terrifies the fearful, animates the courageous.

XLI.

I will obey my parents, honour my superiors, love my equals, respect my inferiors. Wife and children shall be dearer to me than myself. But none of all these, nay, nor all these shall be prized by me like *Truth*. Nay, what are all these if truth be wanting, which is the ligament that binds all these together ?

XLII.

Little wit serves to flatter with, for *how easily* do they work *that go with the grain*.

XLIII.

Of great *vainglory*, but small *virtue* is that man that steals the praise of *other men's* actions, by relating them *as his own*. But these beggarly *borrowers* always prove ignominious bankrupts at last.

XLIV.

A *sick* man distastes those *meats* which in *health* he delighted in ; so those that have formerly *loved* and *delighted* in us, and are now *displeased* with us, even our *best duties do disgust*.

XLV.

To bear crosses and afflictions is the part of Christian resolution, yet *heathen morality* can act it. But to *suffer them* and *be thankful to* God for them, is the sole and peculiar property of admirable Christian faith.

XLVI.

To fear death is always to live in the pangs of death. For most true is it, " Fear is more pain, than pain."

XLVII.

It is worth the observation, to hear the poor man sing to his plough, and the rich man fret in his palace and torment himself. This shows it is the mind, not the fortune, that makes us happy.

XLVIII.

The greatest wisdom of speech is to know when, what, and where to speak ; the time, matter, manner. The next to it is silence. For though silence seldom helps, yet sometimes it hath its advantage; but, at the least, it is innocent and leaves us a perfect liberty without incumbrance, when men of many words are entangled.

XLIX.

If we did *as certainly believe*, as we do *frequently*

discourse of *God's Providence* in every action, it would give us *courage* in our enterprises, and patience in our sufferings. For if God have the overruling hand, and I make Him my friend, when the undertaking is for my good, I fear not the power of any adversary, for nothing is able to stand before Him. But when my weak and sinful apprehension desires and endeavours that which *I think good for me, but His most clear wisdom knows is hurtful*, if I miss my desire, there is not only cause of patience, but of thanksgiving.

L.

Our passions are like the seas, that of their own nature will swell and boil, but more if they be agitated with the winds ; and passions are outrageous if moved by external occasions. But as God hath set bounds to those, so we by His assistance should to these. So far they shall go, and no farther.

LI.

The most immediate way of *winning*, is to be *loving. Ama si vis amari.*

LII.

It is not easy to impose the tongue's silence upon the heart's grievance. But yet I would constrain it, because till the importunity of grief were qualified, it would speak of passion rather than of reason.

LIII.

That master is never well served, that does not carry an esteem with his servants. Above all things a master must be careful that his servants be not eyewitnesses of any base or absurd action.

LIV.

Pleasures moderately used are pleasant, but immoderately prove nauseous.

LV.

The same shoe fits not all men's feet, nor the same reason weighs with every man.

LVI.

The froward, peevish disposition is like the wind —no man knows whence the cause of it is, nor whither it goes, nor how long it will last; but while it is, all are troubled with the fearful noise and rumbling it makes.

LVII.

To judge a man without anger, because we never saw him moved, is to say the flint is without fire : which indeed struck against wood or many other things, discovers not its property, but against steel, shows its nature. And no man is tempered against all occasions, though against many, and it may be most.

LVIII.

The Indies have not made the Spaniards rich. Neither is any man made wealthy by abundant comings in, but by the few occasions of spending.

LIX.

Unkindness among friends is like a breach in a garment. Unless timely stopped, it ravels from top to bottom.

LX.

There is an odious spirit in many men, who are better pleased to *detect* a fault, than commend a virtue.

LXI.

None more impatiently suffer injuries than those that are most forward in doing them.

LXII.

That state is happiest and prospers best where the people rather obey the authority of the ancient and fundamental laws, than dispute the wisdom and policy of the first institutors.

LXIII.

It is not the plenty of meat that nourisheth, but a good digestion. Neither is it abundance of wealth that makes us happy, but the discreet using it.

LXIV.

A man hath two ears, and but one tongue ; they say 'tis because he should hear twice before he speak once. A man hath likewise two eyes given him to look on both sides before he goes forward in any enterprise.

LXV.

It is seldom that any man doth hurt himself by patience or silence, but by having revenge many have undone themselves. What if there be just occasion to be angry, yet ever is it best to stay till the heat of our passion be over, because we may err in the measure ; and there is no time lost—we may, if there be just occasion, be angry afterwards.

LXVI.

Those that are wise neglect not to weigh old and common precepts, and to govern themselves by them, whilst others reject them as threadbare, and looking for fresher, accept of worser.

A FEW APHORISMS AND MEDITATIONS ON SACRED SUBJECTS.

LXVII.

The true Christian is the most *valiant*, the most *wise*, man that is.   *Valiant* he is, for his whole life is a *warfare* against the *world*, the *flesh*, and the *devil*. *Wise* and most prudent he is, for he so well expends his *minute* of *time here* that he may *live eternally happy hereafter*.

LXVIII.

God deliver me from the society of those who fear not the infamy of an evil action.

LXIX.

A man may be a good practical moralist and no Christian, but a man cannot be a good Christian and an ill moralist.

LXX.

The life of a little sick infant is as hazardous and hopeless as the safety of a small bark in the sea, unbalanced and without a steersman.   Every wave, though not rough, tosseth and endangereth the safety of it.   But God manifests Himself most where there are least natural means, and by His goodness they are preserved.

LXXI.

Is pain, sickness, and loss so contrary to us ? and
health, wealth, and pleasure so amiable to our nature ?
Here on earth we cannot have the one sort without
the other.   O my God ! make me therefore wise unto
salvation, that I may have always pleasure, and never
pain, health without danger of sickness, an abyss of
wealth without fear of loss.

LXXII.

It is to a Christian consideration one of God's
greatest mercies that *this world* is full of *troubles ;*
for if we so much *court* her now she is *foul*, what
would we do if she were *beautiful ?*   If we take such
pains to gather *thorns* and *thistles*, what would we
do for *figs* and *grapes ?*

LXXIII.

It is the wisdom of a man to be always armed
against casualties, and the advantage of a Christian
man to be best armed.   Our little moment of time is
obvious to many dangers and afflictions, and these
such as one stroke of them is able to kill us, as the
loss of wife the greatest, of children the next, of
estate and fame.   In how many, if not in all, places
do we lie open.   But faith in God's providence that

o

He orders all for the best is a complete armour of
defence; therefore let us never be unharnessed.

LXXIV.

Those trees that grow wild in our fields we *neglect*,
but for those that grow in our garden we observe the
due times of *pruning* and *cutting*. If we be planted
in *God's garden*, we shall be *cut* and *pruned* by
*afflictions, for God chastizeth every one whom He
loveth.*

LXXV.

The first step of that ladder by which a Christian
man ascends to heaven is *humility ;* and he who
means to overleap that, and to ascend by the rest,
ever misseth them and tumbles back with his pre-
sumption.

LXXVI.

No religious duty doth so purify the heart as the
often receiving of the Sacrament, if we do it with
serious examination ; for that house that is oftenest
swept is cleanest.

LXXVII.

Guicciardini* incites his countrymen to their pris-

* Francis Guicciardini was born at Florence, March 6th, 1481. The
son of an eminent lawyer, he was brought up to the same profession,
and attained to its highest honours. He subsequently forsook the law,

tine virtues, remembering them "that to be a Roman
is a most glorious name, if accompanied with virtue,
and their shame is doubled if they forget the honour
and renown of their ancestors." But Christians have
more reasons to inflame their hearts to piety and
zeal, since their comportment is not only exposed to
the view of men and angels, but to a most pure
essence and strict observer, God Himself; and what
possession was ever honoured with better examples
than ours, Christ and His apostles?

LXXVIII.

A Christian of all others must necessarily be the
most merciful man; for he, considering the great
debt of his sins, and his little ability of satisfaction,
and how freely these were satisfied for by another,
how can he be backward in forgiving others that are
culpable to him? Nay, more, the condition of his
pardon stands but by the exercise of his mercy towards
others.

LXXIX.

Often to consider that Christ by His passion hath

---

and became distinguished by his talents as a statesman and general
under the Popes Leo X., Adrian VI., and Clement VII. He was present at the coronation of Charles V. The fame of Guicciardini is most
connected with his literary works, especially his "History of Italy,"
and his treatises, entitled "Considerations of State Affairs," and "Councils and Admonitions." He died May 27, 1540, A.D.—*Chalmers' Bio-
graphical Dictionary.*

not only gained remission of our sins, and absolved our great debt to God and His law, but hath purchased all our right to our worldly blessings and to heaven itself, will make our hearts tender and pliable, not only to forgive our brethren, but to behave ourselves with all Christian bounty towards them.

LXXX.

Religious love is like Solomon's sword. It trieth whether our love be like the natural mother's, that would not have a division made, or the false mother's, that would have the child divided. The pious heart wholly devotes itself to God, but the carnal and hypocritical parts it with God and its own pleasures and advantages. This scrutiny religion makes.

LXXXI.

O Lord, how great is Thy mercy to mankind, that Thou oftentimes withdrawest Thy blessing from strong means, and so makest them ineffectual; and again, Thou inspirest weak helps to effect great matters. This Thou dost, knowing our wicked natures would adore Thy blessings, not Thee; if the ordinary best means should be infallible. And if Thou shouldst never go along with the means, how lazy we should be, and so become loathsome drones in Thy sight.

LXXXII.

If the Deity humbled itself so much as to join with humanity, nay, more, so as to suffer the most servile condition of our nature, what commendation is it of humility, that to be like Him (who thought it no robbery to be equal with God) is to be humble. Lord make me poor, so I may be but rich in humility. Debar me in all other respects, so I may be honoured with this grace.   O let me be indigent in all other things, so I may superabound in this.   Go yet further along with me, my meek Saviour, that this meditation may not be transient, but often serious and effectual.

LXXXIII.

It is admirable that the reward of our imperfect and finite service here shall be perfect and infinite glory hereafter.   But it is impossible to be otherwise (yet not in respect of us, or our desert, but of God), because His mercy being boundless and infinite, should else be terminate, and God's greatest attribute should suffer.   Lord! that I may often contemplate this with admiration, admire with gratefulness, be thankful with love, love with obedience, and obey with cheerfulness.

LXXXIV.

Lord, Thou hast heaped blessings upon me, if Thou

make them true blessings by guiding me in the use
of them.   The Philistines had once Thy ark amongst
them, but it was a sensible curse to them, but to Thy
Israel Thy great mercy.   O make me Thine, otherwise
these blessings will be insensible maledictions : great
occasions to draw me on to sordid, base affections.

LXXXV.

The true Christian man looks not backward, but
forward : not Pharisaically prides himself to see those
that are worse than himself, but encourageth himself
to reach the perfection of the best, stands not still
like mill-posts that rot in the places where they were
set.   All his life is a race, a progression.

LXXXVI.

The life of a Christian, though it be the highest
profession, yet none are so excellent or perfect but
that even by them much is to be learnt and unlearnt.
And here in this world we are always *disciples*—that
is, *learners :* a good lesson to take down our natural
pride, which puffs us up with so much self-conceit
that we think ourselves *rich* and *clothed*, when we
are *miserable* and *naked*.

LXXXVII.

My dear Saviour, inspire me with the true apprehension of Thy infinite *love* towards me, who

descendedst from the top of Majesty to the lowest
degree of servility, didst debase Thyself to exalt me,
clothed Thyself with mortality to invest me with
immortality, wert poor to enrich me, enduredst the
reproach of Thine enemies to reconcile me to Thy
most justly incensed Father.   Could I but truly
conceive but any part of this immense love, I could
not but return more to *Thee,* to *Thine.*   I should
then forget injuries from my weak brethren, love my
most malicious enemies, hate none but those that
undervalue this great goodness, whereas now my
affections are guided by mine own personal interests.

THE END.